RAP

A Juxtaposition of the Eras

V. L. Collins Jr.

Self Published

RAP

Aka RAP JUX

A JUXTAPOSITION OF THE ERAS

A Deeper Look into the Differences in Rap Culture Throughout the Eras

V.L. Collins Jr.

ISBN-13: 978-0-578-76356-9

Cover design by: V. L. Collins Jr.
Library of Congress Control Number:
Printed in the United States of America

This book is dedicated to:
My parents for creating me and instilling my drive to never give up. To my siblings for supporting me in everything that I do. To my children, WG, Christian, Malori, and Emory, I love you all!

CONTENTS

This Book was written as an investigative work by the author to determine if there are any significant differences in each era of rap music. The author avoided using the names of the artists who are written about in this book to circumvent any alleged defamation assumed by said artists. Although the book does delve into an objective nature when topics are written, the author does approach his written opinions subjectively. The information written in this book could be factual or totally fictional. The reader must decide what they believe to be true.

A Special Thank You goes out to my father,

V.L. Collins Sr.

He has been my biggest benefactor and supporter.

A Special Thank You goes out to my mother,

Rosalind Collins

for those summers she made us read novels and

pushed us to be our best in school.

PREFACE

When I completed Rap: A Juxtaposition of the Eras, I thought that there would be no need for this book to have a preface. I figured that the title itself was explanatory and did not need further explanation. As I began the editing process and allowed a few of my literary friends to proofread the book, I got a lot of feedback in return. Most of the feedback was the expected, like: "Using contractions are usually frowned upon!" or "Try to replace some of the swear words with something else!" or "Some of the slang words you used could confuse the reader!" I began to have second thoughts about how I wrote the book. I went back and started changing some of the contractions, and I removed a lot of the cuss words I originally had wrote. I started changing the slang words to words that every English-speaking person could understand. I started omitting sentences and paragraphs that would come across too hood or ghetto. I was halfway through the book and making changes then something came over me. I had a hip-hip epiphany of some sorts.

I realized that the book I had written was about the hip-hop rap culture. I began thinking about the individuals I was writing this book for. I thought about the people I believed who would purchase a copy of the book. It was then that I realized that a book about rap had to include swear words and slang to be complete. A true fan of rap music and hip-hop culture would understand what I was trying to convey in this book. It was really no reason for me to change anything that I had written.

The book was written for individuals who were interested in the rap culture. It is written for individuals who know the history, and for those interested in learning more about it. I know that the message of the book will not be lost in translation because of some slang and cuss words. For the individuals who may not understand or know the meaning of some words, I included a glossary in the back of the book.

I wrote this book with a purpose in mind. I wanted rap fans from the Foundation of rap to the current climate to understand what is common between us. I have come to the realization that most of my peers do not love rap music like I do. I know that some fans of rap may feel that they have outgrown the genre. This book is for those who still love the music, and for those who participate in the culture. I know that a lot of things ain't what it used to be; but some things remain the same. I hope every person who read this book thoroughly enjoys it! This book is for the fan of the culture of rap music!

THE INTRO

I am a rapper! Not only am I a rapper, I am also a father, ex-husband, employee, and loyal friend to a few good people. Have I always wanted to be a rapper? My initial answer to that question is, No! I have not always wanted to be a rapper; but I have always wanted to be an emcee. I grew up in the eighties when rapping was a verb and not a title. An emcee rapped; but he was not just a rapper. An emcee was someone who developed their skill set through the origins of hip hop. An emcee participated in or was knowledgeable of breaking, graffiti, deejaying, and rapping—The Four Elements of Hip-Hop! An emcee or MC (Master of Ceremony) was able to move the crowd with or without music playing in the background. Hip-Hop was birthed in the early seventies by the deprived youth living in the tough streets of New York. It came from the youth, mostly Black and Latin, who were not allowed in the clubs because of their ethnicity. Again, rap was a skill that the emcee did to express himself. These emcees rapped about their environment and the lifestyles they lived or had wished to have lived. These emcees revealed to the world the ills of growing up in the inner cities of New York. They rapped about the injustices that many black and brown people suffered due to the ignorance of racism. They educated us about our untold history! They taught us about our leaders who were not household names. They taught us to be proud of who we are and of our heritage. They taught us that our history goes back further than the Transatlantic Slave Trade. They also taught us that there were religions, other than Christianity, that we could practice. Being an emcee was clearly the bee's knees, the crème de le crème, at some point in hip-hop; and I wanted in!

The emcees of the Foundational Era of rap were the vanguards to many of the disciplines we now practice. I decided to become an emcee because I felt that it was something that gave the black man a sense of identity in a world that he was intentionally blocked out of. I felt a sense of pride when white media started playing hip-hop music on their radio airwaves. I felt like being an emcee was something that a black man could do besides playing sports or selling drugs. I knew that black people had always been the leaders in other music genres; and I began noticing that rap music was following the same trajectory. Consequently, just like the black music of the past, white people always found a way to infiltrate and make it their own. From the early days of rock-and-roll when white acts stole and covered popular songs from black artists and made it their own; to today where the most popular R&B and rap artists are white individuals. Contrarily, Hip-Hop always found a way back to its roots and supplied the founders of the music a way to continue to earn revenue from it.

Today, rap as we know it, is done by individuals who only make popular music. It is done by individuals who have no idea about the culture of hip-hop or the individuals who lead the way for them to do it. There is an old saying that says: If it were easy, everyone would do it; well rap music must be the elemental stage of all music. I say this because it seems that anybody can make a hit record today. If you will, ponder all the one-hit wonders of the rap music industry. These artists make one huge hit record only to never be seen or heard of again. Rap music have always been a culture that the youth carried; but that was only because it was still in its infancy stage. Today, many of the original artists are now aging in the culture and they are being forced out by those in power. It is the only music genre that does not celebrate their elder statesmen. Every other genre of music has fans and new artist who continue to support their elders up until their deaths and thereafter. It is unfortunate that the fans of hip-hop rap music do not continue showing their support after an artist is no longer in the spotlight. Once an artist is no longer popular with the masses, he/she is put out to pasture never to be heard of or seen again.

I grew up break dancing and doing graffiti on the mean streets of New Orleans, LA (NOLA). I know, NOLA is not the first place you think of when reminiscing about the origins of hip-hop. We mimicked the originators of the culture and followed everything the hip-hoppers in New York did. I remember going to the corner stores asking for boxes so we could cut them open to use them as a mat for breakdancing. I learned how to backspin, spin on my head, and many other break dance moves. We paid homage to the originators of the culture by studying what they did before we could add our own spin to it. I never really mastered graffiti writing because it required either stealing or buying spray paint; and my funds were very limited back then. I would eventually start writing raps as many of the local emcees started to develop their own style of rap. I grew up with and around many of the local rap stars in the city. Many of them would eventually gain national notoriety and some would become household names. In New Orleans, we created a version of hip-hop music that would be indigenous to the city. It was called Bounce Music, and many of the local rap artists and musicians would develop their style from it.

At some point at the turn of the 20th century into the 21st; the music we called Rap started to change. It had become more mainstream and popular amongst the populace. Now, Rap was in every medium of entertainment and the edge it once had was now gone. The suits had taken over, and capitalism had rubbed its hands all over the Rap music industry. The new artists in the game boast and bragged about their criminal backgrounds. No longer was it good enough for the emcee to tell a story about the crimes that they saw; they had to really live and come from a criminal background. Keeping it Real became the taste of the day and you were considered faking it if you did not live what you rapped about. As the criminals in hip-hop became more celebrated by the fans of the music, the suits felt pressured to find more artists with that type of background. Eventually, doing crime was not good enough, you had to be the victim or perpetrator of violence to be taken serious in the Rap game. It was becoming clear that the new Rap artists did not have to come from a hip-hop background.

Hip-Hop as we knew it was no longer a prerequisite for a rapper to get into the game! That thing the emcee did was now becoming what the emcee was. This is when the emcee would take a backseat to the rapper! The suits began to look for any artists with a semblance of rap talent with real criminal backgrounds. This would eventually lead to artists who had no idea about the originators of hip-hop music. These new criminal rappers only had to know how to rap, and that was enough for the suits to put money behind them to make money. Once the drug hustlers in the neighborhood began to realize that is was so easy to get in the rap game, many of them began to invest their drug monies into the rap game. The drug dealers would eventually pick up the microphone and tell their stories about their drug dealing ordeals. Most of these ex-drug dealers were notably not good rappers. Some of them even boasted that they were not rappers; but just good at talking the game. No one in the camp had enough balls to tell these ex-drug dealing rappers about their inability to rap; mainly because most of them were the CEOs of the rap company.

This era would bring in the Swag rappers. These rappers had very little technical rhyme skills, and many of them knew they were not considered good rappers. The rappers of this era were more into the fashion of the moment and their raps resembled this. It was a bunch of sing-a-longs and hooks centered around doing a certain dance that drove the music of this era. Several groups in the South rose to temporary stardom in this "do-a-dance" era. Most of the music was made strictly for the clubs and strip clubs. This era also opened the door for many of the individual "fuck boys" who came to prominence around this time. It seemed like every other week, one of these pretty "fuck" boy rappers were getting their chains snatched. The following week, the local goon would appear online wearing the same chain that was snatched from that said rapper.

Most of these rappers had no sense of where the music came from or who were the forefathers of it. This was due to the suits who controlled the direction of the music industry. It was also because many of these rappers were the first generation of crack babies to enter the rap scene.

The next big thing to blow up was the era of drug dealing or trapping, as it was affectionately called in the Atlanta rap music scene. This era did have many bright stars from the Atlanta area who would continue to pay homage to those that came before them; but it also allowed the less talented artists to sneak in and get shine. Many of the less talented artists jumped at the notion that they could also become famous rappers by talking about their drug escapades over music. This started a snowball effect of any and everybody starting to believe that they could be a famous rapper. The music became more commercialized and less about subject matter with substance. It opened the door for white rappers to infiltrate and become more successful than the wannabe black artists. Today "Mumble Rap" has taken over the youth and is getting most of the play on the radio airwaves. It is called Mumble rap, by its detractors, because the average listener is not properly trained to understand the words these rappers are saying. I know that the music is based mostly on the use of drugs or selling them. When the song is not about drug use; then the sexualization of the opposite sex is the main topic.

As time passed, the hip-hop culture would continue to change. Some would say for the better, while others would say for the worse. I turn on my satellite radio station and most of the songs labeled hip-hop are actually R&B. I noticed that something was changing with the music! Hip-Hop started to grow up and glow up; but the old heads (older fans) were only accustomed to the type of Rap music they grew up on. Simultaneously, the younger generation made a concerted effort to change the music to make it their own. It has been an ongoing feud between the younger and the older generation of rap music for a couple of decades now. The old heads argue that the younger rappers are messing up the integrity of the culture. While the younger generation argue that the old heads are only angry because their time has passed, and the younger generation is making more money than most of them had ever seen. This debate is subjective to each demographic because the music is so different. Technology has played a huge part in the way music is made. Consequently, the rap business is different, and it is much easier to get your music heard.

I decided to observe the current landscape of artists making rap music today. I realized that the music labeled as rap consisted of a diverse group of people. These rap artists were from different backgrounds and ethnicities. Some of the artists did a variation style of rap music, while others did more singing than rhyming. Many of the rap music pundits, like myself, began feeling acrimonious about the state of rap music. I began to become the old man cursing the kids to get off my lawn. I found myself searching for new rap music to listen to that would stimulate me mentally while simultaneously making my head nod feverishly to a trunk-knocking beat. Well, I could tell you, it was not hard finding a hard beat to bop my head to; but finding some soul-searching lyrics became tedious. Every time I would hear about a new artist, I would listen to some of their music and ended up unimpressed. Contrarily, a few new artists have made me pay attention to them. I could hear their respect for those who came before them, and their respect of the artform. These artists have studied the forefathers of the music and often honor them when they rap. I am pretty sure you know of these few artists with very strong rhyming ability, content, and subject matter. I exclude these artists from the plethora of "same-sounding" Rappers of today. I exclude them because they are good at what they do, and they are not just doing rap music … these artists are students of hip-hop! Unfortunately, it is not enough of them.

So, instead of being the get off my lawn old guy; I decided to try and understand the new music of the current rap artists. After all, I have four kids who are growing up listening to these artists; and I needed to overstand what they are listening to. I wanted to know why they felt the need to turn-up for everything. I wanted to know why some continued to rap about using drugs; but would deny drug use in their interviews. After studying their culture with laser focus, I realized that these new age Rap artists had their own culture behind the music. They had a new prerequisite to live by before making it in the rap game. Then it dawned on me, they had created their own elements to the music they did. Just like hip-hop consists of four elements and the subcultures of those elements; new-age rap had developed something similar. So, I decided to breakdown the new age-rap elements. To be consistent with hip-hop, I created or observed the four most important elements of the New Age rappers. The four most vital elements I noticed are: **Drug Culture, Criminality, Attention, and Popularity.** These four **New-Aged Elements** all consist of subcultures within each element. These New-Aged elements are only related to the "Rap" artists within the Hip-Hop community—*Not Breakers, Graffiti Artists, or Deejaying.* Consequently, *one must keep in mind that the New-Aged elements listed derived from the current rap era.* In addition, I must mention that, like hip-hop, you don't have to participate in all four to be in the new-aged rap game; but you must be knowledgeable of each.

So, I began doing research to write the book. As I dug deeper and deeper; I started to notice that the 4-elements I had discovered for this current culture had existed, in some form, throughout the history of rap music. I thought deeper and realized that it would not be fair to pin these four newly discovered elements on the new generation only. It was then that I decided to go back, as far as I could remember, to see how much of these 4-elements had been a part of the generations before the current one. To do this, I decided to do a side-by-side comparison observation about the new-aged elements I created.

I figured the best way to do this would be chronologically. I went back to the origins of rap music and worked my way up to the present. To do this; I had to breakup the past into different eras to properly discuss what was happening in each. My earliest memory of rap was when I was still too young to comprehend the lyrics. I went back to a time when I was able to recite the lyrics; and this was the year 1984. Clearly, 1984 is not the beginning of rap; but it is as far back as I can witness. It is said that hip hop, in its present form, started back in 1973, but the first rap songs on the radio was 1979; therefore, I labeled anything from 1979 to 1988 the Foundation of rap music. From the years 1988 through 1998, I labeled these years as the Golden Era of rap music. I know many of rap aficionado will probably disagree with the timeframe I label as the "Golden Era" of rap; but it is the timeframe I relate to the most. Consequently, it is the time that rap music really exploded and gained universal notoriety. The next era I labeled as the Millennial Era; and this era reigned from 1998 through 2012. I believe that the Millennial Era lasted so long because it was the first era that saw the offspring of the Foundational Era artists make their footprint in the rap industry. In addition, the Golden Era rappers were still producing a lot of music during this era. The last and present era I created is called the "Zoomer" Era. The word Zoomer came from the letter Z in "Generation Z". My assumption is that the Zoomers are supposed to be the revitalized version of the Baby Boomer generation. So, here is a breakdown of the Eras below:

Foundational Era = 1979 through 1988
Golden Era = 1988 through 1998
Millennial Era = 1998 through 2012
Zoomer Era = 2012 through Current

This book will breakdown and explain each of the four New-Aged elements of rap. These New-Aged elements are: *Drug Culture, Criminality, Attention, Popularity*. I will first discuss and explain each of the cultures and subcultures within the culture. After giving a thorough explanation of each New-Aged element; I will then go into each era discussing if and how much of the element was present during that time. I will discuss any subcultures within the elements and discuss what was happening within the culture during each time-period or era. To do this, I listened to the top Rap artist and their music from each era. I watched movies and read articles and periodicals from each era to give me an idea of what was happening during that time. Most of the information was taken from the popular artists of the era. I understand and know that the underground scene influences what becomes popular; but there is more information on the popular rap artists. Although I do not reference or mention the artist or the information sources in this book; I challenge anyone to refute my research. I should also note that I believe that an era is defined by those in control during that time. In the hip-hop element of Rap, the culture is usually defined by the youth. I know that most of the successful rap artists cross several if not all eras of rap music. I focused on what made each era different; and checked to see if those new-aged rap elements were present.

I wrote the book, not to disparage those who practice and participate in today's rap game; but, to give us old heads an idea about why and how they move. After this book is published, I welcome open discussion from the hip-hop community as well as the new-age rap community. I want to develop healthy dialogue and discuss why there is a separation between the youth and those that came before them. I want the hip-hop purveyors to realize that the youth of today are moving differently, and many of them are not doing hip-hop styled rap anymore. I also want to honor the youth who are doing hip-hop because they are carrying the torch into the next generation. So, without further ado, I give you: *Rap: A Juxtaposition of the Eras.*

NEW AGE ELEMENT I:

Drug Culture

TRACK #1: HISTORICAL DRUG USE IN MUSIC

Drugs have been a subject in all genres of music for as far back as I can remember. Many of the jazz bebop artists indulged in their drug of choice back when Jim Crow was still ruining the country. Drug use would cross musical genres where the blues and rock n roll artists would also partake in heavy drugs. Many of these artists would succumb to the temptation of their drug of choice which often lead to their untimely demise. Throughout the 20th century, drugs use has been associated with the music profession. From R&B divas to old aged punk rockers, drugs have been a part of the music making process. So, it should come as no surprise that the artists of the youngest music genre would mimic their elders and indulge in their favorite drug of choice. In the late eighties and early nineties, the drug of choice for most young rap artists was marijuana; or weed, green, bud, or whatever you choose to call it. This was a change from the sixties when most secular music artist chose heroine as their favorite vice of escapism from the real world. Or the seventies when these same artists indulged themselves with the white nose candy and psychedelics that Hollywood's elite partook in. As the eighties rolled in and hip-hop became more palatable to the masses, marijuana became the drug of choice to the youth in America. Many new artists would come in the rap game boasting about the alluring effects of marijuana. These artists would make a career out of rapping about their love of the plant.

Before marijuana would wear the crown as the first drug many youths would use; there was another more addictive drug they usually partook in before they attempted marijuana. This drug was much more addictive, and more dangerous to their overall health. It was looked at as something that only the cool kids did. The actors on television would inhale its smoke and slowly release a plume of coolness in the air between spouting their rehearsed lines. The propaganda would start in early Hollywood. It would then spread to the average working-class man through huge marketing and advertisement. The lingering effects of long-term use was not made privy to the masses in the middle decades of the 20th century. It would not become known that this addictive drug could cause cancer until sometime in the eighties. The drug I am speaking about are cigarettes! For most children cigarettes were the first attempt at mimicking what they saw the adults doing. Like sex, it was something that parents did not want their kids to do before they reached a certain age of maturity. Consequently, just like sex, many children were intrigued with doing something they thought they were restricted from doing. So, when momma asked you to go and light her cigarette from the burner on the stove top, the temptation was too much for you to not take a toke.

Many children would steal cigarettes from an adult; or get an older kid or neighborhood wino to buy some for them. For many of the youths, taking their first puff of a cigarette was their passage into adulthood. The inducing effects of the nicotine became too addictive for many of the youths to stop. Once the habit was formed, many would go on into adulthood with a self-inflicted problem with only themselves to blame. As a youth, I remember the "bad" kids in school were the first to smoke openly in front of their peers. They wanted everyone to know that, along with their behavior, they also were not afraid to do something considered taboo. These prepubescent troublemakers would go on to become the baby gangsters of the neighborhood. Many of them would become the first to succumb to smoking marijuana. They would also be the first to sell drugs in their community. They became the shiny suit in the window that you walked pass every day; but did not realize why you thought that you had to have that suit. They were the peer pressure conduits who would guide you into the annals of the underworld. You were almost induced into becoming one of them. It was as if you had no other choice but to succumb to what they were showcasing. The allure of cool was too much to not participate with the "in" crowd. This coming-of-age would continue through adolescence. This is when the wide-eyed teen searched for the next coolest thing to be a part of. This is when, as a teen, you believed that you were invincible. This is when you realized that some of the stuff your parents told you were to just scare you away from certain things. The more adventurous the teen, the more chances they would take. These, overly confident, too smart for my parents, risk taking teens would be the first to try risqué activities. Two of the thing's parents feared the most for their kids were teenage pregnancy and drugs! For many of the first generation of hip-hoppers, marijuana was the first "real" or illegal drug that they would eventually try.

Marijuana emerged as the drug of choice to hip-hoppers the same way the music itself started. Many of the popstars of the seventies used and talked about cocaine in their music. The cocaine, back then, was a more expensive drug than it is today. It was a drug that the affluent used and it was not too affordable for the hip-hop kids in the ghettos of America. As the rappers of that era began to make money; they wanted to flaunt their success by rapping about using and buying cocaine. Many of the artist back then used cocaine in their rap names or monikers around the hood to separate themselves from the less affluent. The rappers of the early eighties made songs about the cocaine they could afford. It was another way of showing the underprivileged that they were able to afford to live like the wealthy whites who refused their entrance into the ritzy disco clubs in New York. So, just like these same ghetto kids of New York would create their own music spots to hang out and perform their raps; marijuana also followed them because it was something they could afford.

Weed was a way for these kids to experience some of the mind-altering highs many of the white kids indulged in, but for a much cheaper price. Back in those days, weed could be found in every nook and cranny of the ghettos. Most of the kids back then had a relative who openly smoked weed or parents who casually smoked once the kids were down for the night. If you did not have a close relative who smoked, all you had to do was walk to the corner store at night and somebody would be smoking weed along your journey. We all knew a kid who would steal weed from their parent's stash and brought it to school to smoke. For most of us, it was a close relative or elder OG in the hood who would introduce us to smoking weed. In my city back in the eighties, the hustlers who sold weed would sell 3 for $5 joints, "Jernts" or "puffies" as some affectionately called the pre-rolled marijuana sticks. They sold nickel, dime, and $20 bags of weed. If you purchased any amount more, you were considered a hustler. The house parties that your parents had was usually smoked filled from cigarette and weed smoke. I guess no one knew or cared about the dangers of secondhand smoking back then. The kids would be in the back bedroom watching TV as the party went on throughout the night. This was also an economical way many of the people in the black communities would find a way to party for cheap. There were no one to babysit the children because all the possible babysitters were at the party. So, the adults with children brought their kids to the party and we all piled in that backroom to watch what was on network television. At the end of the night, barring no incidents popped off, the kids were awakened from their second-hand weed and tobacco smoke induced sleep, and walked through the night air to their houses. Many siblings were made on nights like these.

Consequently, marijuana became the drug of choice for the youth in hip-hop. It became a way to bond with your peers. For some, it became a stepping-stone into much deeper darker drugs. Some of the marijuana users became enamored with feeling high all the time and many of them would graduate to something stronger. For the most part, in the eighties, many of the hip-hop artists of that time stayed away from the harder drugs. Sure, the white rock-n-roll artists would indulge in cocaine, heroin, angel dust, and many other mind-altering drugs; but these drugs were not easily accessible in black neighborhoods. Black jazz artists in the early bebop era used heroin and cocaine manly because they had a diverse fan base who would introduce them to these alternative drugs. Many jazz musicians would eventually succumb to drug addiction. Famous rock singers, both black and white, would also get caught up in addiction. Sadly, many would die from overdosing on some type of drug. Fortunately for the hip-hop community in the eighties, the harder drugs had become associated with the white musicians. These hard drugs became taboo amongst the hip-hop youth. They became something that junkies or fiends would only use. To be a youth on heroin in the eighties was mostly unheard of.

The fascination of marijuana would continue to grow with the hip-hop youth throughout the eighties. The hip-hop artists rapped about their use of marijuana on almost every record that came out back then. As the eighties passed its midpoint, hip-hop would take a trip to the opposite side of the United States. Enters ... The West Coast! In the latter part of the decade, west coast music took off into the stratosphere. West coast artist, of that time, rapped about the gang violence and crooked cops. The music was aggressive and in your face. It expressed how the street kids on the West felt about what was going on in their "so called" community. The West coast artist rapped about the horrible living conditions they grew up in. These artists brought gang culture into the living rooms of Middle America. Through their lens we learned about what it was like growing up on the West ... particularly California. It was around the early eighties that crack cocaine would show up in the black ghettos of California! It changed the trajectory of our lives!

Crack hit the black community like how the levee waters

of Hurricane Katrina suspiciously rumbled through the ghettos of New Orleans! Crack was a cheaper version of cocaine with a much more addictive high. Users of crack were venomously called: Crack Heads! These crack heads were the people of the community who were supposed to be the neighborhood leaders. Instead, the generation of black people living through this epidemic would lose valuable years of their lives. Many of them were already parents to little children who would grow up without the proper care and guidance of their mothers and fathers. Even worse, some of these children would be born to parents who were avid crack users. The children born from the crack heads would be labeled "crack babies"! These crack babies would lead the next generation of hip-hoppers and bring us to the current state of hip-hop!

TRACK #2: FOUNDATIONAL ERA OF DRUGS
(The Foundational Era)

Before crack was implanted, users would free base their cocaine to get the same high as crack. The freebasing process was much more tedious and dangerous. It involved the use of ether to remove the base from the cocaine. Ether is a highly flammable substance that would cause many users to cause unintentional fires. The freebase process would give its users a quick and very intense high before crashing back down. With the invent of crack, users could easily light up their glass pipes to get their high within minutes. The freebase user would no longer have to go through the tedious freebasing process to get the same high. Crack cocaine was basically premade freebase cocaine. Crack allowed the user to have easy access to the drug. It allowed the users to light up almost anywhere without having to freebase the cocaine. It was cheaper because it used less cocaine to make the product. It was also more popular because you could find it on any corner in the poor black communities.

During this time Rap music was just beginning to take form as its own discipline. It was the late seventies and disco music still held a firm footprint in popular music culture. The DJs were still playing disco music or something with a similar dance driven beat. Around 1979, the first rap record would make the charts. The rap songs during this era mostly had "disco-esque" sounding tracks with shallow lyrical content. The rap songs that charted mostly talked about how much better their rhymes juxtapose their peers. Or, they rapped about topics centered around partying or making people party. It was the beginning of a new style of music, and the rappers were just starting to master their craft. In fact, 1979 could possibly be disco music's biggest year. In 1979, a rap record or artist did not chart in the top 40 on Billboard. Rap had entered at the tail end of a decade that was driven by music that made you dance. The topics of the rap songs had to cover what was popular just to trojan horse the genre into the music arena. As the Foundational Era would continue, the content of the music and subject matter would get much denser as the decade unfolded.

Caveat Interlude:
Before I continue, I must add a caveat about the rappers who would become household names. It is now known that some of the earlier famous rappers stole a lot of their material from better, lesser known rappers in their community. Stealing other rapper's material would later become frowned upon in the hip-hop community. Yet, during the Foundational Era of rap, it was more about who heard the lyrics first. Around this time, it was more about spreading the message so that the rap genre could be taken seriously. I hear that underground standup comedians share the same sentiment about someone copying their material and making it popular first.

As the Foundational era would continue, rap music begun to form its own style of lyricism. It was much different than the popular music of its time. Many of the critics during this era, believed that rap music was a fad; and that it would not last. Contrary to their beliefs, rap music got better, and the lyrical content became more relatable to the rapper's lifestyle! In the early eighties rap music artists were still making music for the breakers to dance to. The subject matter was still based on topics relatable to the lifestyles of the average American family's trials and tribulations. Basically, anyone could relate to the subject matter! This was also when the music started changing structurally and became more about reporting what was going on in the ghettos of America! The rappers began to really talk about what was happening in their communities. This included: social injustices, impoverished communities, and the effects of using drugs!

The early 80s, rappers started making more songs about what was going on in their neighborhoods. Unfortunately for many rappers entering the game, many of them came from very impoverished communities. New York in the early 80s was infused with street gangs and blighted properties throughout the city. This was especially true in the Bronx, New York. The city was searching for a new sound as the 70s disco sound began to fade. It was around the year 1982 when we first started to hear rappers talk about what was really going on in their communities. This is when the talk of drug use was being heard in the records. The rappers of the Foundational Era mostly warned about the dangers of using drugs. We must keep in mind that the 80s music scene was about making pop records; therefore, it would not have been advantageous for a rapper to make socially conscious music back then. So, these songs would not have been the record labels choice to put on radio. So, the early 80s would mostly have songs talking about their rapping braggadocios prowess and lyrics to make you dance to.

As the era would age, the rap music was still reporting about the dangers of drug use. Although most rappers were known for partying; they decided not to boast about what they personally partook in on record. Towards the odes of the decade, the music became more detailed and the mention of drugs started to appear more in rap songs. This was the start of the crack epidemic; and those rappers who made socially conscious music could not ignore what they were witnessing in their communities. The music started to become more sinister as the rest of the world became aware of rap music. We began hearing music from artists in other impoverished communities throughout the United States. Once the artist in the West coast, particularly California, started making records; the veil was lifted! They began reporting on what they were seeing in their drug laden communities. This was the height of the crack era; and as reporters, it was the rapper's job to tell it like it is.

TRACK #3: THE HISTORY OF CRACK

C rack dealers would become the leaders of the community. They would be the people that many hard-working parents would go to when they were in desperate need for money. Many mothers lost their spouses because their spouses had become addicted to crack. Some families would lose their mothers to crack addiction as well. Even worse, some would lose both parents to the highly addicted allure of crack. The few men who were able to navigate death or prison, succumbed to their addictions. This left the hood full of single mothers to raise the children who were born addicted to crack. These crack babies would grow up looking for a male figure to teach them how to navigate through the dangers of the hood. These crack babies looked for strong male role models anywhere they could find one. Unfortunately, it was the neighborhood drug dealer who would appeal to the young crack born youth. The drug dealer carried himself in a way that looked appealing to young impressionable children. It is easy to see why an entire generation of young black males grew up wanting to be a part of the drug industry.

Crack was everywhere in the eighties. The young men who sold crack were locked up and giving long-term jail sentences. Guys would go in as teens and if they survived; come out as middle-aged men. Those who were able to come home on short sentences had usually been vetted to be informants. Crack tore the family in pieces and left the children to fend for themselves. These children would grow up to become victims of neglect. Some of these crack-parent victims grew up in fear of becoming addicts themselves. They grew up hating any form of addiction. The thoughts of being genetically predisposed to addiction lingered in the backs of their minds. Then they were others who would fall victim to drug or alcohol addiction. Many of them would pick up their vices from watching their parents indulge when they were kids. Crack seemed more addictive than any drug I have ever seen in my lifetime. The drug had its victims stealing from their love ones to buy it. Many of the electronics and family heirlooms went missing if there was a crack addict living in the house. I once witnessed a crack head carrying an entire dining room set on his head. He had a round wooden table turned upside down with four chairs sitting in the middle. He carried it up the block trying to sell it to any of the hustlers on the corner who would purchase it. Most parents who could not afford video game systems would put in their orders with the neighborhood crack head. These crack heads became professional cat burglars to obtain booty for them to pirate for drugs. Once they stole something worth selling, they would buy their crack, smoke, and get high; then start all over again looking for something they could steal for their fix. This cycle was not a day-to-day, it was a 24/7 around the clock hourly mission that they repeated by the second. Crack addiction was the first pandemic I had ever witnessed up close.

TRACK #4: THE GOLDEN ERA OF CRACK RAP
(The Golden Era)

The popularity of drug dealing in rap music continued in the early 90s. This can be attributed to why so many rappers in the nineties rapped about crack and its effect on the black community. Rappers were either rapping about selling crack, or how it had terrorized their communities. The irony behind the crack is that the government was "allegedly" responsible for flooding the black ghettos with the drug. (For more information on the alleged government's role search: Iran Contra Scandal) Then, turn around and arrest the same people they provided the crack to. During the late 80s rap music began to change its subject matter drastically. Mind you, there were rappers spitting conscious, positive, and militant minded rap that was intentionally ignored for gangster rap. The West coast rappers started to make noise; and the mediums that played rap music became more bi-coastal friendly. New music video shows allowed users to call-in by phone to request certain videos. This allowed artist, outside of New York, to get national recognition. This is when we started hearing music from artists in different parts of the country. The West coast and Southern region artist would make music that was vastly grimier than their East coast brethren. Well, if not grimier, the lyrics were less metaphorical and more direct. This is when we started to hear songs about crack dealers serving their crackhead customers.

The drug dealing subject matter would continue

throughout the Golden Era of rap music. In fact, it became more grandiose as the 80s rolled into the 90s. Rappers not only rapped about dealing drugs to their local crack addicts; but also boasted about the amounts of drugs they sold. It was no longer good to just sling "dime rocks" to the neighborhood fiends. Now, rappers were talking about scoring eight balls, quarters, and ounces of crack to sell. Some even began to talk about taking trips out-of-state to purchase kilos of cocaine at a discount. The more materialistic the subject matter, the more drugs the rapper had to sell in a song. The idea was to get the listener to believe that he acquired his material treasures from hustling drugs in the streets. It was the true rags-to-riches story line being spewed in these rap songs.

The early 90s saw the emergence of black men becoming CEOs of their own rap labels. The deeper we go into the Golden Era of rap; the more kingpin rap songs became. It can be stated that many of the boutique rap label CEOs obtained their startup money from the profit of selling narcotics. Some might can say that these CEOs were themselves once prominent figures in their neighborhood drug trade. This was a time when we started to hear music from every region in the United States. There were black ran labels in the East, West, and various parts of the South. The Southern rap moguls particularly benefited from starting their own independent labels. They were able to bring their street hustle to the independent rap music game. These Southern Rap Moguls crowbarred their way into a thriving rap industry. They made local rap stars into household names through their independent grind. This is when the rap world began to hear the drug laden stories from the perspective of the Southern street hustler. Many of the rap songs from the Southern rappers had a rags-to-riches theme behind them. The Southern artists rap songs were grittier and based on their reality growing up in the heated ghettos of the South. While on the East coast of the rap world, many of the rap stars rapped about the "Big Willey" lifestyle of the drug dealer who sold weight. Around this time, the West coast biggest artists started rapping about smoking weed and "macking" hoes. These Golden Era artists would continue to make similar rap music up through the end of the era. The Millennial Era would see a paradigm shift as the artists could no longer paint a picture about the street life; but now it was becoming a prerequisite to have lived the life you were rapping about!

The Golden Era also saw the reemergence of marijuana as the recreational drug of choice! As the West coast rappers began to blowup, the talk of using marijuana was dispersed throughout their music. Lyrics about the euphoric feel marijuana gave its users helped push the cool factor about marijuana use. Soon, smoking blunts was being done by rappers on all coast. In addition, merchandise with marijuana flowers became very popular amongst the youth. The East coast and Southern rappers followed with tales about weed driven escapades. It was a big cloud of smoke-filled music being played by the DJs in the clubs. The entire state of California would become known for having the best marijuana money could buy. Simultaneously, East coast rappers still popularized certain marijuana dealers for the potency of the weed they sold. Contrarily, having the good weed was a West coast thing; and many of the rap artists from that coast would rap about the wonders of the plant in their music.

Caveat Interlude:

I must add another caveat to the Golden Era of Rap music. Around this time there was a subculture of conscious rap music bubbling beneath the surface of the more popular rap music. Simultaneously, these rap artists had carved out a niche for themselves to make a living doing rap music. Many college kids, like myself, gravitated towards these artists because we felt they were spitting a more sophisticated version of what the street hustlers were spitting. I personally thought I was special because I was able to understand their lyrics and my hood potnas just could not. I was wrong because most of my hood potnas were just-as or more intelligent than I was. They just did not relate to the sound of the music. This can be proven because they were plenty gangster rappers who made socially conscious rap songs; and their core fans loved it!

TRACK #5: HUSTLE GAME

Hip-Hop would benefit from the crack dealing entrepreneurs looking to invest their money into something other than material items. Many of these street pharmacists would start local record labels with the hope of making it big. The dope dealers wanted to find a legal exit strategy and many of them looked to the music industry as a way out. The kingpins who entered the rap game looked at it as another way to wash some of their illegal drug money. The drug dealers would look at their artists as investments and would use the same street hustle in the music industry. These aspiring CEO's would scour the neighborhoods looking for the best emcees on the block. They promised them fortune, fame, and a way out of the hood. As with most of the youth in the ghettos, these artists jumped at the opportunity to make some money and become famous. Most of the artists who signed to these labels were not too business savvy. Many of them had very little formal education; and were not accustomed to reading legal contracts. They were not paid well in comparison to the amount of revenue their music provided the company. These companies basically practiced a form of predatory lending. By the time they realized that they were getting mistreated, it was already too late to do anything about it. So, although many had acquired the fame they were chasing, many of them ended up broke.

The artists became the reporters of the ghettos they grew up in. They brought their experiences of growing up in the hood into their music. For many of the youth, growing up in the crack era of hip-hop; rap music introduced them to their first image of what a drug dealer looked like. Artists painted detailed images of the daily struggles most drug dealers had to go through. The stories were told from an eyewitness account, and they glamorized the profession of selling drugs. The material spoils that came with selling drugs was enough to lure in many aspiring youths looking for a way to make some money for themselves. Drugs became an easy way for the youth to make a quick buck to support their material wants. For other kids, the propaganda the media pushed about drugs was enough to keep them from getting involved. Contrarily, for these others, the allure was just too much for them to resist. A lot of the youth who did decide to enter the game really had no other outlet to get the money they needed.

Scarcity of the bare necessities have always been a mainstay in the ghetto. One can assume that the same is true of any ghetto regardless of the ethnic group who resides there. I can only speak definitively about the ghettos I grew up in … which were mostly Black. Yet, I can honestly say that growing up in New Orleans we did not separate from other dark melanin filled people. I went to school with black people with Hispanic roots from Hispanic and Caribbean countries. They were considered and treated like the other black people in the community. There was also a strong mulatto presence in the city who had origins dating back to the Louisiana Purchase. In addition, there were several Black Native Americans with history of family living in the area before Columbus arrived. We lived with each other; and saw no need to separate ourselves from one another. Some of the Mulatto families flaunted their fair skin around the city like a badge of honor. They were considered Black and was treated just the same by Whites and other ethnicities outside of the black communities. It was not until I was able to leave my community that I realized that other races consider all people with color black. Colorism was a major issue growing up in NOLA; but I digress; and will leave that for another time or book.

As we entered the 1990's, many of the kids who grew up

with crack addicted parents were now adults themselves. They entered the hip-hop game with the same hustle they observed from the dealers in their communities. They also started to rap about what they witnessed growing up in crack riddled communities. The music began to be immersed with the lives these second-generation crack barons knew. The music became less about partying and having a good time; to detailed tails of poverty and crime. The phrase, "Keeping it Real" would surface as a prerequisite to becoming a rap artist. Now every emcee was an ex-drug dealer or grew up in a drug riddled community. Every song was about the trials of growing up poor in a crack filled community. Gangster rap quickly emerged through the hip-hop industry like a brush fire. What started out as a spark was now a full ablaze fire.

The emergence of gangster rap was like a gift and a curse to the hip-hop community. On one hand, hip-hop was becoming mainstream and more accepted worldwide. This was good for everyone in the rap music business because everyone, including the artists, made more money. This allowed these starving artists to be able to truly feed their families from their craft. Contrarily, it was also a curse because the world now saw every black person through the eyes of the rap stars they saw on television. Hip-Hop rap was being televised worldwide and the images it presented portrayed negative stereotypes about the black man in America. We were no longer rapping about putting an end to violence or going to a party to pick up a nice girl. The images were dark and violent in the music we exported to other parts of the world. Being a gangster was now normalized in the eyes of the everyday citizen. But it also gave law enforcement incentive to harm the black man. Many negative stereotypes were formed from the rap music videos. Every young black male became a thug or had the potential to be one in the eyes of the world. This placed a target on the backs of the young black male who was already seen as a predator in the eyes of white America.

This era in hip-hop rap music was not particularly good for the white rap artists looking to get into the rap music business. These second-generation crack era rappers told tales that only eyewitnesses could account for. The aspiring white rap artists, who grew up listening to rap music, were mostly from the suburbs. Many of them had never seen a ghetto with their own eyes or, for some, had not been in the presence of an actual black person. Or, if they did grow up in an impoverished environment, their family and friends were probably extremely racist towards black people, thus keeping them sheltered and separated. So, when the rappers began rapping about the hardships, they experienced in the hoods they grew up in; many of their white fans could only envision what they were rapping about. The music was now dark and intense; and you could only speak about it if you lived or witnessed what was happening. The rapper became the reporters of what was going on in the ghettos to the entire nation. Of course, wealthy whites and those with political power knew exactly what was happening in the black ghettos of America. They were the ones responsible for putting the crack in the black community in the first place. So, with the subject matter changing to specifically what was going on in the black communities; aspiring white rappers had no way to enter the rap market.

Caveat Interlude:
Throughout the history of rap music, there were and have been white rappers in the game. Some more successful than others. Some were able to crossover into the black communities, while others were not. At some point of the white rapper's career he realizes that it is no longer advantageous for him to cater to the black rap fan. He then makes a 360 pivot and turn his back on the black sounding rap to now cater to his white fanbase. This usually happens after the white rapper has amassed enough success to boldly walk away from what lead him to his success. I likened the white rap artist's venture into the world of rap to the black scholar's venture into Corporate America! Like the white artist, the black scholar must pretend to be someone other than himself to fit in with the culture of Corporate America. The difference between the two is that the black scholar

does not take what he learns and leave Corporate America to start his own business. Instead, he reprograms his brain to believe that he is different than those in his old community and does whatever it takes to remain in his corporate situation!

The negative images in the videos became the backdrop to how rap fans believed all rappers lived. White kids around the nation began to glorify the negative images they saw on television from the rappers. This really painted rap music in a negative light with parents of those white suburban kids. Many of these suburban kids learned about sex and drugs from the lyrics of some of the rap songs. Of course, it would be asinine to think that all white kids' debauchery was learned through rap music; but it was enough of them to put a negative spin on the music genre. The government became involved because now the music they deemed as black ghetto music was now affecting their children. The country became enraged about the subject matter in the music and claimed that it was the cause of the violence in the community. Other concerned parents, of the white middleclass, began to voice their concerns with the subject matter of the music. Feminists, both black and white, joined the movement to condemn gangster rap. They accused the music of being misogynistic. Social and political leaders started campaigns to stop gangster rap music. Record labels, everywhere, started to be held accountable for the music their artists created and put out to the public. There was nowhere for any of them to hide their hands because they were responsible for putting out the music.

The protests and detractors did not stop the music makers from creating songs filled with misogyny, drugs, and violence! The attention that most of the rappers were getting, around this time, only made the suits at the label demand more of the same. If one company realized that another one was profiting from a certain style or content; then they would demand more of the same from the artist on their labels. If the artists did not comply, then the label would drop them and find new artists that would. This was the beginning of all mainstream rap sounding the same. The rappers on the East coast began to follow the West coast artists by creating their version of gangster music. The music created by the East coast artists was a little more polished in the delivery of the content. This approach brought a specific part of the hip-hop music genre to an end. It allowed other artist to "Bite" another artists style to create similar styled music. Biting, or copying another rapper's style, was forbidden in the beginning of rap. The allure for money trumped having authenticity! Nevertheless, it was infused with tales of what many of them grew up observing from their street pharmacists. The drug game was a little different on the East coast than it was on the West. Most of the drugs were usually being controlled by a few figure heads who ran the community on the East coast. Down South, the drug trade moved faster than on the East or West coast. The drugs down South were sold at cheaper rates mainly because of how plentiful it was down there. This could be because of the Southern water ports and peninsula's that saw key loads of cocaine being imported by boat and plane from Mexico, South America, and the Caribbean.

Caveat Interlude:

In NOLA, where I grew up, the drug game was almost an "every man for himself" trade. I remember almost every other hustler I knew eventually attempted to be the supplier of the community at one point in time. I also remember that every time somebody became known as the "Man" with all the work, he instantly became food for the wolves. Growing up in my hood being a victim of a stickup kid was par for the course. I lived a dichotomy of a scholar by day and a hustler by night. I remember stickup kids hopping out of cars like the jump-out boys did to arrest us. No money-making hustler was safe from a hater attempting to rob him from his earnings. It was a time, during the early 90s in NOLA, where it was extremely dangerous to be in the streets making money. I am thankful that I was able to navigate through the mental and physical subjugation of the ghettos of NOLA.

As the popularity of the music grew more and more, parents began to loosen up their harsh opinions about the music. These second-generation parents had lived through the crack era and some had survived their own addictive stages. Many of them were the first eyewitnesses to the intentional destruction of the black community. Some of them played a part in the destruction of the community by participating in the drug game. So, when their seeds started to flower and grow into young adults, many of these parents felt partly responsible for the conditions their kids had to grow up in. Their guilt would hinder proper parenting thus allowing the children to have more freedom than their parents gave them growing up. The children would take advantage of the freedoms they were given. Many of these children would grow up practically raising themselves because most of their parents were usually too busy working to provide for them. This allowed these kids to venture into several mischievous things they would not have had time for if their parents were around more. Most black parents with stable income worked tirelessly to give their children more than they had. They purchased over-priced sneakers and video game consoles that they could not afford. They subscribed to cable television, so their kids could go to school knowing the latest shows on cable television and not be ridiculed by their peers. Some worked two and three jobs so that their kids could not be ridiculed for not having the latest material things. They bought designer clothes and over protected them from the dangers of the streets. Many parents did this out of love; but some of them were truly ignorant to saving money. Unfortunately, around this time, many of the men from the crack era were either dead or in jail. Consequently, the women of the community had to raise their kids on their own. This would lead to a recipe for disaster. Most of the young men had very little conflict resolution skills. This left a trail of bodies in the street out of ignorance. For many of these kids, they would become the first crack babies spawned from their crack dealing and crack using parents. They would enter the real world with very little know how to feed or protect themselves.

TRACK #6: THEY CAME FROM EVERYWHERE
(The Millennial Era)

As the Golden Era ended and the Millennial Era began, the rappers from the Golden Era was still making hits for the mainstream audience. The Golden Era rappers provided so much powerful music that their impact was still very strong going into the Millennial Era. The Golden Era introduced us to rappers from all coast and made them all household names. Consequently, the Southern and Midwest rap scene exploded as the artists from these regions hustled their way into the top of the rap game. Rap outfits from New Orleans, Atlanta, Tennessee, St. Louis, Houston, and Florida all had emcees who topped the charts during the Millennial Era. It was truly a Southern takeover as the Golden Era East and West coast emcees played a background role to those incoming Southern rappers. The smart rappers, or should I say, true artists from the East and West coast found a way to stay relevant during this time. Some of the biggest artist from these coasts would team-up with the Southern rappers to keep their presence imprinted in the rap game.

As the 90s came to an end and the new millennium materialized, the Southern rappers were on top of the rap world. The music was infused with drug references about marijuana and drinking codeine and promethazine laced soda which was affectionately called syrup or lean. If the West coast artists were responsible for the recreational use of marijuana, the

Southern rap artists did the same for lean. The use of syrup was ubiquitous throughout the South. It could be assumed that the trend started in Houston; but almost every one of the top Southern artists rapped about using syrup in their music. If the song was not about lean or had a bar about it; then you saw the artist drinking it in his video. Lean was usually represented by having two stacked Styrofoam or plastic red cups with a purple-ish colored liquid swirling inside it. Like marijuana use in the Golden Era, Lean was that to the Millennial Era. Eventually, rappers on every coast began to use it as it became popular amongst the youth. Unlike the effects of marijuana, the abuse of Lean was much more detrimental to the human body. This drug affected the body like a liquid heroine. It slowed down the heart rate and made the user feel extremely lethargic. It was an added downer to the weed that most of them had smoked. Unfortunately, we lost some of the biggest names in rap music from the misuse or overuse of Lean.

The Afro American community has always been a petri dish of undiscovered talent. We literally learned to make lemonade out of lemons to survive the trying times we endured throughout the years. The hip-hop artists of the crack era promoted Money Over Everything (MOE) and Bitches Ain't Shit. So, it should come to no surprise that their offspring would follow their same path. The big difference between the crack babies and their parents is that their parents learned how to survive from just observing their parents or other elders in the community. Contrarily, they were not around enough for their offspring to learn anything from them. These kids, most of them, grew up without fathers around to show them how to become a man. The little girls also suffered from a lack of a parental presence because they would mimic what they saw on television. Many of the young women in the music industry also practice the mantra, "Money Ain't a Thing" and they would do whatever it took to acquire it. The boys would grow to become "wannabe" thugs; and the girls "wannabe" vixens. They learned to be who they were from what they saw on television. The boys would stop at nothing to acquire what they deemed status worthy. They would rob, steal, and kill their mothers if it meant that they could shine. The young women would also do extreme things like stripping and hoeing to have material things. We will later see that this behavior would be rewarded in the hip-hop/ rap community.

TRACK #7: THE KIDS ARE WATCHING
(The Zoomer Era)

The turn of the twentieth century saw the rise of the third generation of rap music take center stage. The seeds of the crack babies were now emerging on the scene looking to make some noise of their own. These kids, like their predecessors, searched for something that would make them stand out from the pack. They wanted to create their own identity in the hip-hop music industry. They wanted to leave their mark on history by having their own sound. Of course, this meant going in the opposite direction of their deeply rooted hip-hop parents. In the early 2000s, a new batch of artists emerged as the face of rap music. These artists were a bridge between the 90s era and what we know as rap music today. Fortunately for them, the mainstream radio was still playing some rap music with a little substance. As these artists started to age and the millennials began their ascension through the ranks; some of them felt a need to stay relevant. Unlike other music genres, rap is a young man's sport. So, these older artists felt compelled to make young music to stay relevant in the game. They started making rap songs with subject matter that would attract the younger generation. This ideology is a part of having longevity in the music business.

The marijuana usage did not stop when the popularity of Lean increased. Most guys would sip on their purple drink while simultaneously smoking their favorite strain of weed. Their tolerance would grow, and guys needed more and more of the drug to reach their highs. This was the same way that most crack heads got strung out on crack. It was this chasing of the highest high they could achieve to get the same feeling they had when they first used the drug. It was normal to see young guys at the club nodding off from the effects of the drugs they consumed as the extremely loud music blasted from the speakers. It was only a matter of time before the drugs would begin to influence how the new rap music sounded. The slowed downed dragged out beats resembled the feeling of double downers such as lean and weed combined. One might can say that being in this extremely drugged-out state brought about the sound and style of the Mumble Rapper. This allowed for less talented rappers to come into the rap game and make a name for themselves. The Mumble rap songs were driven by the beat and lyrics were barely understandable. It was a gift from the Millennial Era to the Zoomer Era which made it that much easier to succeed in rap. The garbled sounding lyrics were truly written for those living that lifestyle. In hindsight, it could be said that every rapper in all eras only made music for the people living similar lifestyles.

The Zoomer Era rappers began to mimic their white counterparts, both past and present, from rap and rock music. Particularly the latter musical discipline was more influential to the young Zoomer Era rappers who only wanted to live of life of sex, drugs, and music. The Zoomer Era rappers' infatuation with white rockers helped open the door for more young white rap artists to enter the world of rap. These rappers started to explore different drugs and would also rap about it in their music. They introduced a new way to reach the same high that most of their black counterparts rapped about. In came the use of pills or "popping pills" to the rap artist. At some point the young black artists started to mimic what they thought would be cool in amongst the youth in white America. They began taking all sorts of pills to go along with the lean and weed they were already consuming. MDMA which is short for methylenedioxymethamphetamine or "Molly" began surfacing in the inner circles of many of the young hip-hop communities. It is suppose to be a more potent form of ecstasy. It is a hallucinogen that gave it users a euphoric high. Many users of the drug would feel extremely sensitive to their feelings and emotions. The drugs were taken in a capsule or pill form. The youth would now add this to the cocktail of drugs they were already taking.

The black kids were trying to be accepted by the white kids, simultaneously the white kids did everything possible to learn hip-hop culture from the black kids. Both groups were looking for a way to crossover and be relatable to the other's community. This was happening while most of the white heartland was quietly becoming addicted to opioids. The media did not and has not covered the opioid crisis like they did the crack cocaine epidemic. The only reason I can think of, as to why the opioid crisis is not propagandized like the crack era was, is because most of the opioid users are white. By not reporting on the dangers of the meth users and the effects of using opioids, the media has been complicit in its widespread use. In addition, most addicts of the opioid crisis are given opportunities to rehab and not do exorbitant jail sentences. The lack of reporting on the dangers of opioids made it easier for gullible street kids to accept using them. What was once considered something a weirdo would do, was now considered cool. The new rap artists now had a new drug to go along with their new form of rap music. As popular rap music started coming from artists down South, the type of drugs that were consumed also followed. The music slowed down, and the rap artists needed a drug to slow them down as well.

Popping pills was not a new form of getting high. In the eighties and nineties, individuals would pop a valium, Percocet, acid, or some form of opioid or synthetic drug to get high. These individuals were usually teens from white communities who would raid their parents medicine cabinets to get high. Then at a party when they were first introduced to weed blunts, they would, in return, offer some type of pill that you never experienced before. One could only assume that the pills were stolen from a medicine cabinet because they were not considered illegal. These "medicine cabinet" druggies were mostly from the suburbs. They were considered weirdos in the black community! The difference is that the individuals who were popping pills to get high back then were not considered cool. It was the white rappers who made popping pills cool. The black kids would follow suit and they too began using pills to get high. As per usual, once the black community got involved with anything, it became the cool thing to do amongst the youth. I believe that the black kids' affinity to do what their white brethren were doing was a way for them to separate themselves from what their parents and the generation before them were doing. Black teens began wearing tee shirts of old has-been rock bands just to seem different than their baggy jeaned forefathers.

At some point the way rappers talked about drugs in their music changed. No longer were the raps about the tales of drug dealers and the money that was made from the trade. Instead, the rapper decided to make his music about the effects from the use of the drugs. Again, I believe that this all changed when, mostly Southern, rappers started rapping about the use of Lean in their music. This morphed into the use of more synthetic type drugs and hallucinogens. Also, when the white rappers finally started to make music that black listeners liked, the usage of popping pills became immersed within the culture. It was if a pass was given for the popular kids to now use alternative drugs. This would eventually lead to the Zoomer generation to come into the game rapping about their use of drugs in their music. Art tends to imitate life, consequently, many of the kids growing up listening to the music felt compelled to use the drugs talked about in the music they listened to. So, now the new artists rapped about how high they were getting. They talked about how the drugs influenced young women to be loose and do unusual sexual acts when on the drugs. The lames or the square individuals were now the guys who only used marijuana. The true to the bone hustlers were now looked at like outcasts on the club scene.

TRACK #8: I BE DRUGGED OUT
Aka Generation Pill

Currently, there is a new drug culture amongst the hip-hop youth. The clubs are filled with pill popping, syrup drinking, weed heads who only really care about satisfying themselves in the present. The millennials have decided that instant gratification is better than planting a seed and waiting for fruit to grow. Many of them believe that it is futile to wait for something that you can have today. The problem with this type of thinking is that they do not consider that some things take time to acquire. They also must realize that resources and jobs are scarce, so it is almost impossible for all of them to have the material success they so much desire. The new drugs that they consume are indicative of their "have it now" nature. Long gone are the days of sipping a strong whiskey and a nice cigar to get you to a relaxed state. Even just smoking weed is not enough for this generation. They need to have their highs immediate and strong!

This generation could be known for their love of popping pills. The pharmaceutical medication that has been prescribed for other serious medical issues have been discovered by the youth to use to get them high. Most of these kids began using the pills to get high because they were prescribed for them to help with a diagnosed symptom or illness. These medications are usually used to treat symptoms of depression, autism, or ADD. The kids abuse them and give them cute names like Xannies and Perc's. Most kids do not know or care what the original intent of the pills are for; they just know that it gets them to their desired destination quicker. The rap artist of the Zoomer Era makes music that encourages the use of these pills. The sound of the music is slowed down so that the mind of someone on a drug cocktail can understand. To make matters worse, most young rap artists come into the game without drug addiction or habitual drug use. It is the people in the industry who introduces, encourages, and support their drug habits.

The rap artists of today are using more potent drugs than their hip-hop rap forefathers. The marijuana has more THC, and they are chasing the weed with more drugs. Today kids are "dabbing" or smoking concentrated forms of marijuana in vaporizers and bongs. Like most trends, old or resurfaced, the youth made light of what dabbing is by creating a dance move with the same name. The sound of the music has also changed due to the type of drugs usage of the music makers. No longer do I hear a variety of rap styles on the radio airwaves. I no longer hear different sounding music from each coast. I only hear what these kids are putting out. Even the East and West coast artists are sounding like Southern artists. This partly can be blamed on the original rap artists on the East coast. It was because of their East coast bias that many of the artists from other coast and regions had envy in their hearts. I believe that the fans of the original East coast boom-bap rap were also complicit in other regions feeling some type of way about East coast artists. Of course, if you look back, you will see that the artists themselves were able to put aside their differences. Contrarily, the fans just refused to open their minds to listen to other regions doing the music they help popularize. Therefore, it comes as no surprise that when the other regions began making waves in the music industry, they only looked to put on their coastal brethren before anyone else. This same type of nepotism is what most of the other artists complained about with East coast music labels and radio stations. Eventually, the Southern rappers were much quicker to work with artists from all regions.

Today the backdrop of the music of the new generation of rappers is laden with tales of drug use. The hypnotic drums and dark heavy basslines encouraged the artist to spew lyrics that could complement their sound. The rappers poetically laid lyrics about drugs, violence, and sex. Each region, trying to one-up the other, spawned artists who were more polarizing than the last. Record executives searched feverishly to find new talent to copy whatever the hottest trend was. This copycat method of producing music would ultimately bring forth the discussion that hip-hop was dead. Although payola had always been a part of the music industry; it was now being used to play records that all sounded the same. Southern rap moguls began using their deep pockets to persuade radio programmers to play their music in regions that previously shunned their records. East coast, Mid-West and West coast music executives began to look for artists who sounded like the ones on the radio. The new artists in those regions began adapting to the Southern sound and they created music that was similar.

NEW AGE ELEMENT II:

Criminality

TRACK #9: GANGLAND MENTALITY

At some point in the rap game, it became normalized for any and everybody to join a gang. It was as if well established artists, who were already household names, decided one day that it would be a good idea to join a gang. This could have been due to many artists chasing trends or joining just to have some form of protection. Many of these artists were never affiliated with gang culture; and most of them did not come from a city where gang activity was prevalent. Consequently, these same artists felt compelled to be a part of something they had no idea of how and why it operated. Growing up in the ghettos of New Orleans, gang culture was not a part of our upbringing. Back then, the city was more about every man to himself. The violence was centered around the different wards and certain neighborhoods. The colored bandanas that we wore represented the ward we were from, and not a gang. In hindsight, I guess you could say we did practice the same retaliatory violence that the gangs in LA did; and some of us did represent our wards like that of a gang. Contrarily, we were not organized, and no man had an allegiance to a certain ward. Basically, it was not about where you were from; but mainly about where you were at. Today you see gang culture immersed throughout hip-hop rap culture and in most of the music videos. It is not surprising to see a rap artist, or even a pop artist, doing the Crip Walk in their music videos. Some of the most non-threatening music artists felt it to be safe doing the

Crip walk as a dance in their music videos. The dance itself was one that the real Crip gangs of LA originated. In the late nineties, the gang culture began to be in every ghetto across the United States. It spawned this new era of pseudo gang culture amongst those in the popular hip-hop rap community.

Gangs have been around for as long as I can remember. They have been woven into the fabric of America in some form or fashion from the origins of the country. From as far back as the start of the thirteen colonies, like-minded individuals formed groups to rebel against the system that was in place. Each ethnicity had their own form of gangs. From the Italians and the Irish, to the English Protestants and the Jews; every ethnic group had some organized crime element who controlled the underworld. These groups or gangs felt as if they were locked out of achieving the American dream. So, to get a piece of the pie, they formulated gangs to forcefully take what they wanted. The formulation of ethnic groups coming together to create gangs goes back to the immigrants arriving in New York at Ellis Island. They have been movies that recreated the environment of New York City when the immigrants arrived at Ellis Island. It was a hectic environment of ethnic groups coming together to protect their resources by any means necessary. These men fought, cheated, and killed each other to control and protect what they thought was theirs. It was a time where the immigrants from every country were the poor, and the rich colluded with the criminals to remain in a power position.

The Afro American community would be no different from any other. They too would also form gangs to commit crimes for their own personal gain. The black gangs were in most of the major cities, like Los Angeles, Chicago, and New York. The first time I heard about black men coming together to form a gang, had to be in the early 80s. The city was New York, and the Bronx was burning literally and figuratively. I heard about these gangs, who were mostly made up of Latin and black people, fighting in the mean streets of New

York City. Their wardrobes reminded me of the biker gangs I saw in the movies. They wore leather and jean jackets with their gang logos on the back of them. They fought with bottles, chains, and any type of object they could find to use as a weapon. These gangs were formed to protect their communities and survive through systemic poverty and racism.

The gangs of LA would be the first gangs I became familiar with. This was mainly due to Hollywood glamorizing and putting LA gang culture on front street. I would be remised if I did not mention that the CRIP gang originally meant: Continuous Revolution In Progress. The CRIP's gang original ideology modeled that of the Original Black Panther Party. The criminal element of the Black gangs would really take off in the eighties. The Bloods gang was formulated in the early 70s to protect themselves from the CRIP gang members. The "Robin Hood" effect of the original gangs had long disappeared from the agenda. The youth of the eighties were gang banging with a selfish agenda. Long gone were the days of organizing to bring about positive change and justice in the black community. What was once started to protect their communities had somehow been reversed to terrorize it. One might could say that there were external forces playing a major role in the gang's turnaround. These kids gang banged to have the material things they saw their white peers with on television. They too wanted the video games, clothes, and sneakers that only a few could afford in the hood back in the 80s. So, they would turn what was once positive into a negative to acquire the things they wanted!

The rappers on the West coast would introduce the rest of the world to the modern-day gang life in the black community. They would glamorize gang life as if it were something fun to participate in. Although the lyrics painted an entirely different story, the positive attributes would still shine through the cloudy negative lyrics. The black youth would look at the camaraderie that the West coast gangs portrayed in their music and videos. This portrayal of gang life would eventually make its way to the silver screen and give those interested an inside look at the internal operations of how most gangs operated. It was as if gang culture was given a greenlight in Hollywood because it was seen in almost every form of entertainment media. Now, the youth had an idea of how to start and operate their own gangs within different ghettos throughout the country. Gangs were popping up in every city and town. Small and large towns alike would see a spike in gang activity. The gangs would continue to grow larger and larger under the watchful eye of national law enforcement. What was once considered an activity that was too dangerous to participate in; had now become what most ghetto youth aspired to. The government was taking heed to what was going on; and they also began to watch the gangs more closely. They did not want the gangs in the black communities to develop into the organized crime gangs of the Italian community. So, to combat this, the government enforced stricter laws for those who decided to participate in gang violence.

TRACK #10: LOCAL GANGS?

I remember growing up in New Orleans, we did not have the Crips and Bloods in our neighborhoods. Consequently, we did have our own version of gangs who represented each ward in the Greater New Orleans area. I would have the tough task of growing up in the Third Ward in New Orleans. This area was made up of three of the toughest projects in the Greater New Orleans area. It housed the Magnolia, Calliope, and the Melpomene projects. The area was ridden with daily violence that mostly lead to the murders of young black men. I grew up amongst the chaos, and at times, I also played a small part in the destruction of the community. We had no idea of how bad we were damaging the community of where we lived. We had no idea that family's lives were being destroyed. We had no idea of the lingering hurt that would remain a part of our community. Looking back to the time growing up in my hood, I never felt like it was my job to maintain or protect the community. I believe that this was because most of us were renting and new that our living conditions could change at any moment. We treated the hood like we felt we were being treated by the cops, government, and America in general. We treated our communities like cheap rental cars, because subconsciously, we were aware that we did not own anything. We were treated like savages, therefore we acted accordingly.

Consequently, it was this environment that laid the backdrop for some of the most successful local rap artists in New Orleans. Just as the Bloods and Crips provided the graphic muse for most West coast artists, the projects, wards, and senseless violence did the same in NOLA (New Orleans, LA). Bounce music would rise-up from the bullet shell cases that covered the streets of New Orleans, to having major mainstream artists sampling bounce beats, riffs, and adlibs. These local rap stars would find refuge from the streets through the music. Unfortunately, many of the artists were too deep into the street life; and would eventually succumb to the violence they rapped about in their music. It would not be until the mid-to-late nineties that these local artists would find national success. I too would jump into the fray fresh out of high school by starting and becoming a part of my own rap group. We made some local traction; and would continue to build success up until Katrina. As the local artist of New Orleans became household names; the type of thuggery they engaged in would also expound. These rappers would feel the pressure to become like their more infamous known peers. This mimicking of some of the things the more famous rappers were doing, would eventually make a turn for the worse. They would pick up the same gang culture that was made popular on the West coast.

TRACK #11: WE BEEN THUGGED OUT
(The Foundational Era)

The origins of rap music did not have too many songs boasting about the criminal lifestyle or any gang activity. Although many of the artists in the early 80s came from crime ridden communities, the music they made rarely expressed the criminal element they grew up in. The rap music in the early 80s were more about the rappers displaying their rhyming ability. The artists wanted to be respected as such and they focused their music around making hit records. It was plenty of battle rappers in the beginning of rap who would not go on to see nationwide success. These rappers came from communities where gang banging was prevalent. Artist from the inner cities like Chicago would make their way to New York looking to get signed by one of the major record labels. These artists knew about the gang activity in Chicago; but knew that it was not yet appropriate to rap about such things. Consequently, most aspiring rappers may have had gang riddled raps, but was smart enough to rap about whatever was playing on the radio at the time. As a result, many of the rap stars we would come to know today got their start in the battle rap scene or by mimicking or looking up to a battle rapper. This could be the reason there have been so many notable battles throughout rap's illustrious history.

We all know that rap, coming from the hip-hop culture, got its start on the East coast in New York. The early rap songs were based around the beat patterns which were mostly created by the 808 drum machine. The artists complemented the bass heavy beats with lyrical domination and creative cadences. The early East coast rap was the catalyst for what we heard on radio stations around the country. Many of them became must-haves for cookouts and parties in every community. These were songs that every local DJ played to get the block party started. If one of these songs come on today, we all will know every lyric and beat pattern to a tee. The rap producers of that era probably were influenced by the popular music of the time. The rap songs of the time were designed to make you move and dance. This was a prerequisite to get the DJs to play them in the clubs they worked. As the 80s began to expand, a few DJ lead rap crews would begin changing the message we were used to hearing in rap songs. This opened the door for other rappers around New York and the East coast to add their flavor to the music.

It would be around the year 1985 when the world would hear one of the first gangster rap songs on wax. The music came from the Philadelphia demographic and it would spark artists in different parts of the country to add their tales of gangsterism to the rap game. The flood gates opened, and artists everywhere figured that they too could rap about the gangsters and the gangster lifestyles they grew up watching. Some of these rappers had a front row view to the action, while others lived the lyrics they rapped about. On the West coast the artists were living through the crack epidemic, as was most cities around this time. Yet, the crack epidemic hit the cities of California the hardest because it was being imported to the ghettos of the state. The artists living in Southern Cali all the way up through the Bay area, started making gangster rap records. These records were much more sinister and driven by their environment. Sex, Guns, and Drugs were ubiquitous throughout the ghettos on the West coast during the mid-to-late 80s. This brought heavy attention from the authorities, and police forces began heavily enforcing the law. Crack Task Forces and violent police brutality became the norm for the gangsters and gang members who made their living in the drug trade. The rap artists would begin reporting what they saw on records. Gangster rap music was born, and the trajectory of rap would change forever!

In the 80s our lifestyle was changing into a more socially accepted one driven by fashion and music. The youth in every community listened to rap music and followed the fashion trends of the rappers. As the gangster rap music made its way around the country it would eventually land in the South. During the mid-eighties, the first semblance of gangster music we heard came from Miami, Florida. The gangsterism coming from Miami, FL was not violent like that of LA; it was more sexually provocative. The music was base heavy, and it focused on making women gyrate to the music. As I mentioned earlier, the term "Pussy Popping" came from the music ... today it is known as twerking. The music held no punches talking about the sexual prowess of the male anatomy dominating and penetrating that of the female. I personally remember kids repeating the lyrics to some of the songs and getting kicked out of class in 3rd grade. Just like the gangster rap music coming from California, the Miami rap music had become taboo to have around your parents. I mean, not only was it taboo to play the music; your parents did not want you to own a cassette or vinyl album. I remember getting my cassette copy from a neighborhood friend; and I taped it every time it popped. The music became so infamous that it got the attention of local and national authorities to ban the music from being sold. This was the beginning and the catalyst of Southern rap music!

TRACK #12: LIFE IMITATING ART

The hip-hop rap community was always infatuated with mafia lifestyle. In the 70s and 80s there were several movies made surrounding the lives of the Italian mafia. These movies took us into the lifestyle of the Italian Mafia families that existed throughout the 20th century. They displayed the dangerous, grimy, treacherous, and often glamourous lives that these mobsters lead. These mafia styled movies would lead to movies showing the criminal elements of other ethnicities, such as the Columbians. In the 90s more movies and made-for-cable programs would continue to be released showing a life of crime that was only talked about behind closed doors. Whether these pieces of art were authentic or not, it gave those wanting to live a similar lifestyle an imaginary blueprint. These crime-based movies were very popular in the African American community. Black kids ran around the hood pretending to the be the lead protagonists in the movie they just saw. Some guys would even begin to pick up similar characteristics of the characters they watched in the movies. Guys I grew up with loved the rags-to-riches stories in the gangster movies; and many of them truly believed that, they too, could build similar criminal empires. This longing to be the man turned the city into a violent gumbo of crabs in the pot. No one man could get bigger than the next, at least not knowingly!

During the 80s, they were not too many crime-based movies made specifically about what was going on in the black community. When the 90s rolled in, black people were longing for a gangster style movie with characters that resembled them on the silver screen. Then around 1991, a couple of crime movies made by black producers and directors were released. The movies were an instant smash in the black community and even traditional white movie critics gave them a positive nod. These movies displayed black men as the leading characters playing both hero and villain. Then around 1993 another powerful crime-based movie was released starring two young black actors as the lead protagonists. The movie was extremely violent and influential to the young black youth in the ghettos. This movie, like one of the others released in 1991, showed the dangerous lives of the gang members living in California. It also revealed the fear that the gangs evoked within the subconscious minds of those who were not affiliated. The black crime movies of the 90s had polarizing characters that heavily influenced those infatuated with the gangster lifestyle. I grew up amongst the influenced, and I have seen many come and go attempting to live out a movie. The 90s would continue to produce African American crime-based cinema. The movies influenced an entire generation and implanted something in our spirits.

As a youth I remember how movies and television began to change how some did their dirt in the hood. As I previously mentioned, every ward had a certain color bandana or soldier rag we would wear to represent where we were from. We wore the rags as a form of solidarity to represent what ward we represented. Someone from the 3rd ward could be in the same spot as someone from the 9th ward and not feel any animosity towards one another. After the black crime wave of movies of the 90s, guys started becoming more territorial about the communities they lived in. This "set-tripping" was not limited to only the ward you were from; it was also certain blocks within the community as well. I can remember being fresh off-the-porch in the early 90s and every project or block had their own crew. We felt a sense of camaraderie and thought it was our duty to protect property we did not own. Suddenly the city exploded into a violent cesspool of crime and murder. Young men were robbing and murdering people for designer clothes, shoes, and drugs. Stickup kids were robbing the neighborhood dice games. Drug dealers were setting-up other drug dealers to get robbed for merchandise they had just sold them. Crooked cops extorted, robbed, and killed young men hustling in the streets.

The crime rate in New Orleans during the early 90s had risen to an all-time high. The city was labeled the murder capital of the world around this time. A city already known for its spices had become the hotbed for crime and murder. This upheaval in violence was not limited to just the Uptown area. The Westbank of New Orleans really picked up the gang culture of California; they started wearing flannel shirts and chucks. Downtown projects also were riddled with infamous gunslingers who represented each Downtown project and hood. Drive-by-shootings became a thing in the 90s. I remember guys getting together talking about "riding" on a neighboring hood for what they considered disrespect. Several young black men became contract killers for any local drug dealer who wanted someone killed. Guys would come from rival hoods and rob the dealers in another. This would of course spawn retaliatory reactions from the victims, who would in turn reciprocate the crime. Black bodies were being found around the city and in rural parts of Louisiana. It was truly the killing fields; and I made it out by the grace of God! The 90s in New Orleans was a very volatile crime driven city. I cannot say for sure that the movies of the 90s influenced the crime; but I can say that the criminals resembled the characters we all watched on the silver screen.

Caveat Interlude:

What's Beef? Since the origins of rap music, emcees have always battled one another for supremacy. It was a tribal instinct in us that moved us to want to control out territory and to take control of yours. In fact, all the elements of hip-hop sparred against each other during the foundational years. It was a display of healthy competition and respect for your fellow artists. The B Boys, deejays, and graffiti artists all wanted to be considered the best in their craft. The competition between artists would start by artists first representing their individual hoods. As hip-hop would become more popular, this representation would blossom into reppin your city or town. By the time we heard the record down South, it had developed into artists representing their entire state. The Foundational Era artists all found a way to keep their battles rooted in the art. The battles rarely moved outside of the art. The Foundational Era emcees would also spawn classic battles between neighboring cities in New York. The rap battles during this era would decide who would eventually become the leaders and household names in the rap industry.

TRACK #13: STICKS
AND STONES
(The Golden Era)

I n the late eighties/early nineties, many rappers would pick up where the generation before them left off when they had to settle a dispute on the mic. Rappers would still have a healthy dislike for their competition and would express their disdain for the other through their raps. Whether "sneak dissing" or something more overt, many emcees created beautiful music as an outcome. It was around this time that those battles begun to cause more than just hurt feelings. The tribalism would begin to cause more physical affliction than verbal. At some point in the nineties, the new rappers in the game were more sensitive than their foundational forefathers. The words being said on wax somehow made them take it more personal. No longer did the old 'sticks and stones' adage work for these rappers. The new artist emerging during the early nineties were way more sensitive than the generation of artists before them. The artists in the 90s would step to other artists they had beef with. Yet, the beefs in the nineties and 2000s would remain on wax. This was a time before social media; so, the fans only found out information through word-of-mouth or magazines. For me, this was considered the Golden Era of rap music. Almost every major artist would drop timeless classics during this time.

The Golden Era played the backdrop for one of the most dangerous battles to ever happen in hip-hop. It spawned a real beef between two of the most notable East and the West coast rappers at the time. The beef would force rappers from each coast to pick a side. Although the beef between these artists developed from something personally, each artist settled their differences on wax. East coast rappers had to support artists from the East, and it was the same on the West. In the South, we also choose to ride with a certain coast. I decided not to choose a side because I loved listening to music from the artists on both coasts. The media played a significant part in pouring fuel on the already blazing fire. Artists from either coast found it difficult to travel and perform on the other coast. The fans on these coasts felt that it was their duty to protect their coast. Once again, our tribalism would rear its ugly head! The beef between these two rap artists would end up with both being killed. Still today, their murders remain unsolved!

Caveat Interlude:
What I remember most around this time was that the fans truly supported one coast or the other. In NOLA I can honestly say that we related to the West coast artists more during the verbal wars. As I mentioned above, I was Switzerland, and I supported artists from both coasts. At one point it got so bad that you were badly ridiculed if you pulled up playing any East coast artist who were dissed by the West coast artist. As time would pass, and both of those brothers were murdered, it became less coastal bias. I can only imagine the good music that was missed because you felt the need to support a coast.

The murders of two rap icons was still too macabre for a generation that was raised during a very violent era. It was too much for rap artists from all coasts. Even the West coast artists, who had lived through the apex of gang banging, realized that the beef was taken too far. It would be too late before the leading artists of the time realized that the beef was influenced from outside sources. The media played a huge role in perpetuating the beef between the two coasts. Record sales were at an all-time high for rap artists. The rap game would suffer minorly, and it allowed for other peripheral artists to sneak in and take over. Yet, the rap game would not miss a beat because rap music was still ascending. The music was becoming more popular in the mainstream, and the children of middle-class America still desired its authenticity. So, record execs found artists to replace the deceased; and the ball just kept on rolling.

The crème de la crème of the Golden Era rap artists still made the most impactful music during this time. These were the artist who were babies during the Foundational Era; and had witnessed hip-hop grow into a thriving profitable industry. Before, during, and after the East vs West coast rap wars, artist was dropping classic after classic albums from every point on the map. This was truly a golden time to be into rap music. The rap artists still had a lot of creative control; and the music was still very authentic to the artists. The music covered all areas of rap: lyrical, gangster, conscious, playful, and party. Contrarily, many of the more popular artists still boasted about the criminal element within their music. Due to the talent of these artists, the rap tales became more intricate and believable. It was getting to a point where aspiring artists had to have really lived or had some sort of criminal background. Slowly the Foundational Era artists music faded to the background. Certain GOATS from the Foundational Era was still making impactful music; but the majority had thrown in the towel. Some artists with a limited hood mentality were forced to create rhymes that the gangsters could relate to. Some artists were clever enough to hide conscious messages within their gangster rap tales. These are the artists we look at today as the best of the Golden Era.

In the nineties, rap beef was handled by making the most disrespectful punchlines one could think of to put on record. Rappers would throw subliminal shots at one another on record if they dislike someone. It was not foreign for rappers to confront one another if they happen to be in the same space at the same time. Sometimes the words spoken in the rap songs could trigger strong emotional reactions from the opposition. This would usually require a response record from the opposing emcee. If the emcee refused to respond it was automatically deemed a loss for that person. It was a time when rappers took a diss very serious. It was as if someone had talked about your momma on record, and it was on onsite. Rappers in the Golden Era took dissing as serious as rappers in the Foundational Era took biting. If you dissed a rapper on record, it was certain to attract combat from the opposition. During this era, rappers did not have the luxury to release their music instantly. We had to wait until the rapper released an official album, mix tape, or single before we could hear the response. This allowed the first diss record to gain some traction; and it built up anticipation to hear a response from the opposing artist. This also allowed both rappers to dig up all the dirt they could possibly find on their opponent to put into their songs. Rap fans would wait patiently to hear the response record.

Towards the end of the twentieth century, the rap battles became more vital to the success of an artist career. If a rapper lost a battle, it could have literally ended his career. The court of public opinion determined who would win the battle. A few rappers ended up losing their careers to up and coming rap artists looking to make a name for themselves in the game. These new rappers would throw stones at established artists hoping to invoke a response from said artist. The goal was to get them to respond so that the newer artist could use their name to boost their popularity. This concept became known as "Clout Chasing" when you intentionally tried to insult someone more popular than you in hopes that they would respond. If the more famous person did respond, the less famous person would use the attention to boost their following. This happened to a very popular rap artist around the beginning of the 2000's. The artist was at the top of the rap food chain; and was making very popular radio tunes. He lost a battle to an up and coming artist and his career has not been the same since. The established artist was ambushed by the new artist; and because of the lack of current technology, he could not respond fast enough for the public to hear. By the time he did respond, it was far too late to recover. The new artist would go on to achieve great success, while the established artist continued to fall from grace.

TRACK #14: GLAMOROUS GANG LIFE

G ang culture had become a part of every social platform amongst the hip-hop youth. It was seen in rap videos, rap music video shows, and even in black hip-hop sitcoms and television shows. It had become commercialized and desensitized to the American viewing audience. Sport figures and rap music video personalities had been spotted representing gang culture in some form or fashion. In fact, it had become so immersed in the American culture, that hip-hop vernacular became a major part of the American lexicon. People of all walks of life began using hip-hop verbiage in their everyday language. It is the reason why words like bling are a part of the dictionary you use. So, it should come as no surprise that the youth of today are still infatuated with gang culture.

The idea of belonging to a group is as American as NFL football. We grow up looking to be a part of some form of a group for various reasons. As youths we formed neighborhood clubs, that were innocent in nature, to feel like we belonged to something bigger. This wanting to belong would continue throughout our school age years when we joined sport teams and different committees, and organizations. This would continue in college by joining fraternities and sororities to feel like we just belonged to something bigger. The police in America have their own fraternal order; and many of our politicians belong to some form of secret society club when they were in college. The point is this, the young kid growing up in a ghetto wants to belong to something fraternal to feel some form of camaraderie. Unfortunately for this kid, the neighborhood gang is the only group that he sees who practice this type of coming together.

Many rappers from the Millennial Era are affiliated with gang lifestyle. Unlike their predecessors of the nineties, these new rappers are coming into the game boasting about gang activity with little to no worries about repercussion from law enforcement or retaliation from rival gangs. They wear their gang colors like the latest fashion trends. They boast about killing each other like proud parents do their kid's achievements. Being gang affiliated had become a prerequisite to becoming a major mainstream rap star. Even the more talented newcomers have found a way to speak on thuggery in their music. Many of them have witnessed or have grew up in neighborhoods that were gang infested. These new talented emcees also were old enough to hear the music their parents played from the 80s and 90s. So, they came into the game looking to earn the respect of those that came before them; but simultaneously looked to impress their drugged-out peers. It is a tight-rope act that many artists cannot seem to carry out. It is a small few who had the necessary talent and skills that is required to make it. A small few had the street appeal to still crossover into the mainstream. Those who did, eventually became the household names because the black community could relate to their subject matter as well as those from other ethnic communities.

The affinity for gangster lifestyle did not start with this generation of rap musicians. Their elder peers also incorporated gangster lifestyle in their music and raps. It was the movies in the seventies and eighties, with their gangster and mafioso story lines, that lured the youth into their world. Many rappers in the late eighties and nineties fell in love with the gangster movie storyline. They loved the rags-to-riches story line that many of them envisioned they could eventually ascend to. They incorporated the energy within their own music; and would use some of the actual lines from the movies in their lyrics. As the movers and shakers in Hollywood began to see how the hip-hop community supported these types of movies; they started making similar types staring black actors and protagonists.

The new generation of rappers are also influenced by the crime element that our society offers. They witnessed their elders glorify these movies and attempt to live out some of the story lines. They heard the lyrics of some of the earlier gangster rappers; and studied and mimicked them in the mirror. They saw how even the crossover artists of the time incorporated gangster lyrics in their music. There is no difference in what the youth are doing today. They want to feel larger-than-life and feel like no man can touch them, if only within their music. This type of machismo is a main part of the hip-hop culture. It is a culture that condemns those who are weak and soft. It ridicules any male rapper with a semblance of femininity. Rappers would kill you if someone even accused them of being gay. The nineties were tough on any aspiring rapper who did not follow the rap template: you had to write your own rhymes, you could not bite or steal someone else' rhymes, and you could not be homosexual. This prerequisite for new rappers would continue up into the 2000's. Then all, of sudden there was a shift.

The early 2000's saw East coast rappers sounding more like Southern rappers. The South had been popping for more than a decade and rappers from other regions were looking for ways to capitalize on the South's sound. Of course, rappers on the East and West coast still had the underground artists and the veterans who remained true to their sound; but it was still hard for these artists to go pop in the new era of rap music. New emcees began to shy away from the rules of the game. They started to do their own thing; and ignored what the rappers did a decade earlier. They realized that the new sound was in the South; and they wanted a piece of the action. These new artists began to create a sound that resembled what the rappers in the South were doing. Rappers from the East and West coast had chart topping records that mimicked popular Southern Do-My-Dance and sing-along type songs. Those who were more creative was able to mesh their regional sound with the trap drum patterns of Southern rap. What would emerge was artists from different regions creating a new sound that allowed each of them to work with one another. The beefing that prior generations saw was no longer being accepted within the circle of the new artists. Those who lead the charge in this generation were eager to work with their brethren. The tribal idea of rappers only working with artists from their region was gone. The new wave had arrived, and they reveled in being different than the generation before them.

TRACK #15: PIMPING AIN'T EASY

They say that prostitution is the world's oldest profession. If this is true, then pimping must follow by a close second. Just picture: A caveman with a stable of women he turned-out by allowing other cavemen to have their way with them for a payment in freshly caught wild game...But I digress! Pimping has been around for as long as I can remember. I reckoned at some point in the history of prostitution a pimp became necessary as a form of protection from the prostitute's Johns. The Blaxploitation movies of the 70s captured the essence of pimping and hoeing in the inner cities of America. They glamourized the pimp as a winning figure and community leader that black people in the ghettos should aspire to become. In the 70s there were not too many positive black images on the silver screen. So, naturally young black boys would leave the cinema wondering how they too could live the life of a pimp. If they did not openly admit their admiration, the idea was already supplanted in their subconscious. In these movies the pimp was living the American dream; they drove luxury cars, wore the flyest threads, and openly had sexual relations with white women. These accoutrements were coveted or taboo in the black community. Consequently, the success of these movies in the black ghettos were inevitable.

Rappers were always looking for the most attractive thing to rap about in their music. They searched for what they thought would be appealing to the masses of rap likeminded fans. Most of us in the black ghettos were infatuated with any rags-to-riches story that involved criminal activity. The pimp was the classic example a man starting out with nothing but his mouth and his intellect. With his ability to sell young poor girls dreams, a pimp was able to build him a stable of women to work for him. These women willingly gave the pimp their money because they were convinced that they wanted him to have the best of everything. In turn, the pimp would provide them food, shelter, clothing, and protection. Thus, based on the compounding of the money given to him, the pimp was able to amass a massive amount of wealth. Well, his wealth was massive relative to where he was living.

The pimp, like other criminal hood pundits, became a topic of many rap songs throughout the history of rap. In fact, many rap artists centered their personas around that of a pimp. These rappers would enter the game spittin tales of the pimp lifestyle while simultaneously wearing matching pimp attire. They embraced their album covers decked out like a pimp would if he could rap. Most of these pimp-styled rappers came from the left coast. The Southern rappers would also eventually come out with their version of pimp styled rapping. In the 90s songs about pimping started to appear on the charts; this acquired topic would continue through the 2000s. Rappers helped push the idea of pimping into the everyday square lifestyle. Soon you would see young boys treating young girls they encountered like the hoes talked about in the music. It became cool to have more than one girlfriend. Contrarily, you were looked at as a simp if you only had one girlfriend and treated her with respect. It became a numbers game, literally and figuratively. As a teen we would go to school dances or to block parties and second lines to see how many phone numbers we could collect from the girls. This was well before we all carried cellphones on our person. At the end of the day, the guy with the most phone numbers were considered the man. We all respected him and looked up to him hoping to one day be in his position.

As a youth I remember wanting to have just one pretty girl

I could have as a girlfriend. I would sit in my 4th grade classroom daydreaming about the prettiest girl in the school. I knew she had a boy that she already liked; yet I fantasized about her still. As the seasons passed and I would graduate to middle school, my interests in many things would change. No longer was my favorite music the soul music my parents played in the house. I began listening to the music my peers favored. This music was rap and it literally took over my subconscious. I no longer wanted to rap for only entertainment purposes, I now listened to and studied what the rappers were saying. I figured that the rappers could teach me something because most of them were older than I was. Simultaneously, I began paying more attention to the upper classmen and older cats around my hood. I believed everything I heard from both the rap records and the older kids on my block. I hung around the porch as the older heads held court and reminisced about their glory days. They discussed everything from politics to police brutality; but when it came to women, I quickly learned the more the merrier. The rap music expressed the same sentiment when it came to women. Rappers called women bitches and hoes; and encouraged us to treat them all like hookers. If you want them, get them, even if that meant you had to pay for it.

Fast forward to the present landscape of rap music today; the songs encourage misogyny and polyamorous relationships. Both women and men have been conditioned to believe that "hooking up" is the standard relationship requirement these days. Gone are the days of courting a woman to get to know if she is worth your time. The kids today are pressured by their peers to have sex with one another with no intellectual attachment. The girls who are not putting out—Must—to be considered by the guy they like. If she does not, then surely another girl of his liking will. The girls who are willing to hook up become enemies of those who are less promiscuous than they are. Young people are losing their innocence at a much earlier age. Information is so easily acquired that nothing is left to the imagination. So, who is to blame? Is it the pimp game, Hollywood, or the music industry? Is it just how things naturally progressed?

TRACK #16: THE CRIMINAL MILLENNIALS
(The Millennial Era)

Around the turn of the twentieth century, two of the Golden Era of rap biggest artists would clash. They would create the most viscous lyrically beef we had heard since the mid-nineties. This time it would be two artists from the same coast who would lock horns. Fans would again choose sides as to whom they thought won the rap battle. For some it was the artist who drew first blood; but many others believed that the response from the other artist was much better. It all started when one of the artists would mention the other in one of his most vociferous songs on his album. Sources close to the two artists believed that the battle was spawned from something personal between the two; but to the fans, we only followed what was said on the records. The other artist would take offense; and would come back with his own diss track on his album that release months later. Thus, a rap battle was sparked between the two. Fortunately for both artists, and the rap fans, this battle would remain on wax. It would birth two of the greatest diss records in the history of hip hop! The winner of the battle would be determined by the fans. The subjective nature of choosing a winner allowed for a different winner based on who you would ask. Both rappers would go on to work with each other in the future; and both would have extremely successful careers outside of rap. Either way, the two artists had taken over the attention of the rap fan with diss tracks that were far from ethereal!

As the 90s ended and the new millennium quickly approached, rap music had become the number one genre in the world. To uphold the number one spot in music, the sound had to evolve to satisfy both the hardcore rap fan and the casual. Rap records had to have a sound that spoke to its base and still crossover to a pop audience. The gangster rappers continued to have a stronghold on the charts in the 2000s. They began collaborating with music producers who had the ability to make crossover appealing music. Thus, we started to hear more upbeat tracks with gangster raps over them. Of course, we know that cream rises, so it should be of no surprise that the best songs were created by the best rappers. The end of the Golden Era brought in some fresh blood to the rap music industry. These new rappers entered the game with the same aggressive rhyme style as those that came before. Yet, something was different about the sound of the gangster music that was being produced. The lyrics were still very thuggish; but the music provided a more polished sound than the producers from the Golden Era. These new producers had mastered making music with crossover appeal. The sound was a culmination of the rawness of the 80s and the 808s of the 90s, with melodic synthetic sound beds driven by deep base rhythms we could dance to. These new producers were not from the East or West coast as most were accustomed to; they were from the South, particularly the Virginia area.

Today rap beef is different than it was the generation before. Rappers are willingly working together to make hit records. I applaud the millennials for deciding to put aside their differences to work with one another. This newly kumbaya of rappers working together was a shock to most from the Golden Era who were accustomed to rappers beefing with one another. Back then the beef could have spawned for several reasons. In the origins of rap, beef mostly would start from someone biting another rappers rap style; or dissing a demographic of where they lived. In the following generation of rappers, beef became a way for lesser known rappers to make a name for themselves. The Golden Era rappers would start beef over almost anything; and nothing or no one was off limits. The beef would jump off if someone assumed you were talking bad on their name in a record, even if the diss was subliminal! The most trivial misunderstanding cold morph into something humongous. Unfortunately, some very macabre lyrics would speak themselves into existence; and some of our best emcee's lives would end violently during that era.

As time would pass and technology would improve; rappers started having the ability to release records overnight to respond to a diss record. If a rapper dissed someone on a record on Tuesday, a response was expected no later than Wednesday. It is to the point that the longer it takes for one to respond to a diss record, the less effective it becomes. As we crossed into the 2010s a new era of rap began to crystalize. It was the seeds of the Golden Era rappers entering into the rap profession. Yet, like the eras before, rappers who started in the prior era was reaching their apex in the newer era. A good example of how quickly one can now respond to a beef happened in 2015. In 2015 two of the top Millennial Era rappers faced off in a mediocre rap battle. The first artist made a comment on a social media platform about the other artist's not writing his own lyrics. As you know in hip hop, a true emcee should never use a ghostwriter? Well, in the Foundational Era of rap, ghostwriters were not allowed; but, one of the first rap hit songs had lyrics that were stolen from another rapper...But I digress! The rapper in question immediately released a diss record within a few days after the social media message was released. One can assume that the quick diss record response was to prove that he wrote his own lyrics; but this too can still be debatable. The rapper who made the social media message hesitated to respond to the diss record; and before long the other rapper had released another diss record. With two diss records aimed at the social media comment rapper, the fans wanted to know if he would release a response diss record. He did eventually release a mediocre response diss record under the pressure from the fans. Unfortunately for him, the fans automatically deemed the rapper who released back-to-back diss records the winner of the rap battle because of the former's late response. Once the fans decided who the winner was, it was nothing the social media rap artist could do to change their minds. Fortunately for the artist, his career would continue to blossom beside the loss he took on wax.

TRACK #17: CHILDREN ARE OUR FUTURE
(The Zoomer Era)

The offspring of the crack generation grew up wanting to be like the neighborhood movers and shakers. They wanted to be like the only people they could relate to success. In their eyes, the drug dealer, the athlete, and the musician (particularly rappers) were the people they yearned to be like. They would master the art of mimicry and would practice doing exactly what they saw their idols doing. Unfortunately for them, these people were the only people they saw who look like them who were successful. They were no black doctors or lawyers who decided to stick around the community. Most of the African Americans who earned any success quickly moved away from the neighborhood they grew up in. This was and is a learned behavior for many black successful educated individuals. For most of these black intellectuals became bourgeois and linked up with other individuals just like them. Truly, the Talented Tenth did not have time to implement a 10-Point System; they were too busy running away. As a matter of fact, it is encouraged to disassociate yourself from humble beginnings so you can fit in with your peers in academia. So, most of the kids growing up in the black ghettos had few positive role models because they all moved away.

These kids became the future drug dealers of the community. The drug dealer, the athlete, and rapper were the only professionals close enough for them to eyewitness. Some

TRACK #17: CHILDREN ARE OUR FUTURE

of them blessed with athletic ability were immediately scooped up by the local AAU coach and put on the fast track to becoming a professional athlete. Those who were literate enough to formulate their words through rhymes would become the next aspiring rappers in the hood. For the others, they would become career criminals who would spend their youthful years in-and-out of the prison system that was waiting on them to slip up. Those who choose not to be a part of crime or had no affinity for sports or music ended up working menial jobs. Consequently, some of the mentally challenged kids born to non-crack addicted parents ended up just living off their government checks. Mental illness linked to drugs or natural selection usually went undetected. These kids grew up with parents who had zero parenting skills. They would be the future killers of the community because they had no guidance or disciplinarian to guide them. I had many associates I grew up with who, in hindsight, had some type of mental illness. They learned to act like the rest of us and did just enough to look "normal". I would eventually realize that some of things they did would not be considered normal by anyone living outside our community.

These mentally challenged crack kids were willing to do whatever it took to "get-on" in the rap music industry. Some even believed that you had to do a crime to be considered legitimate. The phrase, "Keeping it Real" would become the slogan many of these wannabe thugs practiced. They interpreted the phrase to mean that you had to do or be involved in what you were rapping about to be considered "real". If it was discovered that you were not actually living the life you rapped about; you were considered a fraud, fake, or phony. The term "Reality" rap would emerge as a genre within the hip-hop industry. The Reality rappers were either ex-drug kingpins or currently living the life they portrayed in their raps. It became a thing to say that, "I actually live it!" for rappers coming into the game. There was an influx of new artist entering the game who were involved in some form of criminal activity. These new artists would boast about being shot and selling drugs prior to entering the rap game. Many of them claimed that the music was a way for them to escape their criminal lifestyle. They would do interviews and always manage to bring up their criminal past without even being asked. Several artists that you hear on radio today were birthed from this era of the rap game.

Today, these same rappers still rap about the drugs and violence in their music. Many of them are well into their thirties and early forties and have exhibited no growth in their subject matter. Sad part about this is that a lot of the "so called" reality rappers are lying about their involvement in criminal activity. Some of them only got involved to help bolster their rap careers, while others become victims of their newfound celebrity. Some of these rappers would be arrested for the first time after becoming famous, they did not foresee the consequences before committing the senseless acts they thought necessary to maintain their personas. Some may argue that the fame helped shed light on their existing criminal activity; while others knew that they were coerced into a new life of crime. Very few of these rappers were really involved in what they rap about; but none of them did nothing to make their fans aware of their falsehoods. Rap had become a caricature of itself; and it was only beginning to grow larger. The effects of the crack era were now bearing fruit and the hip-hop rap community was beginning to feel the brunt of it.

The teenaged kids of the Golden Era artist were now the freshmen class entering into the rap game. Generation Z or Zoomers is the name that is given to this generation. I coined them the Zoomer Era of rap music as we are now currently living through this era. At some point during the Millennial Era of rap music, it became mandatory for an artist to have come from or lived a criminal background. This would continue into the Zoomer Era of rap; but there were some subtle differences about their criminal history. The Zoomer Era rappers had witnessed how the wannabe gangster rappers of the Millennial Era had suffered from pretending to be something they were not. During the Millennial Era of rap, many posers had to deal with real life circumstances. Some of these rappers were robbed for their jewelry; did jail time; and some were even killed. These Zoomer Era rappers, a few generations removed from the hardships of the Foundational Era rappers, lived a way more comfortable lifestyle. Yet many of them are aware of the social injustices of the past, few of them can truly empathize with the suffering. So, to combat the drama that comes along with being a poser, these extremely intelligent kids decided to change the paradigm about what it is to be a gangster rapper. Now instead of talking about selling drugs and busting guns, these kids began rapping about using large amounts of drugs. The gangster was now the one who could pop a molly or perc, drink lean; and smoke weed with high amounts of THC. As with every prior rap era, to stay relevant, you must incorporate what the current era is talking about in your music. As a result, many of the Golden and Millennial era artists drop lines about "popping a pill" in their music.

The weed that our parents smoked in the seventies is not the same weed that the current Zoomer Era artists are smoking in their videos. The weed from the sixties and seventies was called reefer and was grown with no additives. The amounts of THC were not as high as it is in the bud being smoked today. The THC in the weed the rappers smoked in the nineties and till this day, was much higher than what was found in our parents' flower. The drug got you much higher and is more addictive. Independent marijuana growers began creating stronger strains of the drug to give you a much stronger high. Each new strain developed came with its own street name. This made it easier to identify what type of weed you were purchasing. Some of the strains were named for their color, i.e. purple, or, because of how it was grown, i.e. hydro. Each weed strain gave you a different type of high. Some was more medicinal, while others were designed to get you high fast. This new weed created a market for the hustlers to sell weed as the entrée in their smorgasbord of drugs.

In the 90s, because of the West coast's musical resurgence

about the flower, marijuana started being sold at a premium. The marijuana was now medicinal, and growers started creating different strains of the drug as if they were chemists. The nickel bags spiked to the same price as a dub sack, and all hustlers claimed to have had the California light-green fluffy weed flown in, whenever one complained about the price. At that time, you still had a choice to purchase some Reggie or get you some Dro for about $10 a gram. Mind you, at the time, we had no idea of what type of weed we were buying. It could have been sativa, Indica and any type of high THC strain; but you paid more because it was not Reggie. When the new weed strains first hit my hood, everyone claimed to have had Indo for sale. Then the next strain was Hydro, and Purple quickly followed. It was always that one kid who went away for the summer and he would come back claiming to have a strain we never smoked before. He would come back home for the fall saying stuff like, "I got some of dat East coast Chocolate Thai" or "I got dat Hawaiian shit that'll make you feel like you floatin!" Most of the time the blunts were already rolled, so we really did not know what strain we were smoking. We never questioned the contents of what was inside the blunt; we were just happy to be smoking some of the same weed that the rappers we looked up to smoked; or so we thought.

TRACK #18: MOB (MONEY OVER BITCHES) MENTALITY

The hip-hop artists of the 90s ushered in the MOB (Money Over Bitches) and the 'Bitches Ain't Shit' ideology into rap music. This would ultimately create an entire generation of artists who would make similar music denigrating women to be less than. The women they rapped about in the music were objectified as only a sexual being to be used and tossed away when done. The music would teach the upcoming generation that women should only be used for sex and nothing else! The women would become disposable to the up and coming young males who looked at their favorite rapper as a role model. Many of the inner-city boys only had their favorite male rap artists to look up to for a positive male influence. Simultaneously, the record labels had stop promoting rappers who made uplifting and positive music. The music was stripped of having any semblance of what it takes to be a man. The artists who rapped about uplifting the black man no longer had the support of the record labels. Ultimately, these artists would find themselves being pushed to the underground and going the indie route. This new direction in rap music would help in minimizing any new artists from creating positive rap. Kids looking to get into the music industry was forced to make music about female degradation if they wanted to get heard by the powers that be. In addition, the music videos helped in creating the image of what a loose woman should look like. As a result, the young girls of the community were also influenced by the images in these music videos.

The Black woman would take the brunt of the negative blows being thrown at them through the music. The propagandized images being shown through Hollywood and the media helped to emblazon negative stereotypes in the brains of the ruling class in America. The images people saw on TV helped shape their opinions about every decision they had to make in their lives. The television programing subconsciously placed the ideals they wanted to push in the minds of the people. The influence of these programs is so powerful that multinational corporations pay millions of advertising dollars just to appear on their airwaves. These companies understand how hypnotic visual images are. They hire advertising firms to make the most polarizing commercials they can think of. Unfortunately, in the Black community in the 90s, many girls would become sexually experienced well before the girls of the prior generation. Although it was still frowned upon, teenage pregnancy had become more normalized in our community. In fact, I will credit music for individuals openly discussing what they did in the bedroom. The generation before me, the Foundational Era of rap, barely discussed what they did with a woman in bed, or at the least, it wasn't as graphic. I remember graduating from high school and a few girls were already pregnant; back then, teenage pregnancy was still sort of taboo. As the years would pass the girls would begin getting pregnant at a much younger age. With the systemic decrease of strong black fathers in the community, the young girls had a very limited number of positive male role models to look up to. So naturally, they looked to the positive images they saw in their communities. Unfortunately for them, many of the males in the community mimicked who and what they saw on television. As is commonplace with any race of people; you gravitate towards the images that look like you. For the young black males in the ghetto; those images were of the rappers in the music videos.

The acronym for Money Over Bitches spelled MOB, could have also been interpreted as some type of affiliation with the crime underworld. Some rap outfits claim that MOB was based on crime affiliation. Either way, those letters indicated something that was not positive for the community; and many kids grew up under the influence of the artists who rapped about it. MOB became the mantra for every "so-called" hustler in the game. Every young boy growing up in the ghetto placed money on a pedestal while looking down on their women. This would eventually give those on the outside looking in a green light to attack the women in our communities. The rappers painted vivid pictures of debauchery and promiscuity with women they did not know. They implanted the belief that making money was more important than being monogamous or just respectful of the female gender. They ushered in the phrase "booty call" indicating that sex was the only reason for getting together with their female counterpart. Booty calls would eventually give way to "hooking up" which was a term that bridged into the next generation of rappers.

The millennials took this idea of MOB to higher heights. They rapped about girls giving fellatio as commonplace as a handshake. Hooking up became a prerequisite to determine if the relationship would grow legs. Girls would learn to become sexually active at younger ages just to keep up with the Joneses. The music also became more sexually overt. In the Foundational Era, rappers wrote lyrics about women that left something to the imagination. By the time the Golden Era arrived, women became bitches and hoes on record. The Millennial Era rappers encouraged the sex before dating culture. No longer did rappers imply or simply use other words to paint the picture of what they wanted from a female partner. They put direct messages in their music to let their female counterparts know what was required and expected from them. In the nineties, rappers talked about bitches and tricks who carried themselves like bitches and tricks. Contrarily, the millennials made bitches synonymous with every female. Therefore, daughters, mothers, aunties, and grannies all became bitches in their eyes. Today the Zoomer Era rappers just continues to support the themes that were created by those that came before them. They no longer ask for sexual favors, they now state "when" are you going to do it. Now it is like: If I communicate with you, I need to know when you are going to perform fellatio on me; not if. Consequently, the young girls have now adopted the same behavior as the men. Many women of the Zoomer generation have found ways to tap into their masculine energy. These young women only want men to appease their sexual desires and nothing else. Women are now calling themselves "Alpha" and, because they no longer need men for income, they can now approach the ideal of sex just like a man would. This could be due to several reasons; but that is another story for another book.

As a result of the promiscuous behavior by both genders, more kids are having unprotected sex. According to the CDC young people from the ages of 15-24 make up more than half of the new STD cases. One must believe that at some point these kids started to believe that they would not or could not catch a deadly STD; or they just did not care. It is the clear case of the youth believing in their invincibility. It is my conjecture that the youth of the Foundational Era of rap music dealt with the scare of catching HIV or AIDS to have frivolous unprotected sex. As we moved into the Golden Era of rap music, the artists were still a little shook from the AIDS epidemic and promoting unprotected sex was still not a thing to do. Also, many guys knew a guy who was struggling because of child support payments; thus, causing the male populace to practice safer sex. Somewhere between the Golden Era and the Millennial Era rappers started to talk more reckless about their sexual escapades. It started with girls bragging or dragging about their male counterpart's pullout game being strong or weak. Like most trends within our community, I first heard about pulling out in modern day blaxploitation movies and in rap songs. I started hearing guys talking about "going raw" inside females when they had sex, and not being afraid because they were able to "pull-out" right before ejaculating. Guys started making excuses about not liking condoms or that they were allergic to latex. Today the young folks have the morning after pill to prevent unwanted parentship; but nothing yet has been invented to stop the spread of STDs. I don't want to pontificate about safe sex; but I urge all young men to think about the lives they could affect when they skeet inside a woman.

TRACK #19: INTERNET BEEFING

The millennial artist in the current generation have taken their beefs to the cyber world! Internet beefing is now a thing with the millennials and their peer counterparts. The Zoomer Era rappers have picked up where the Millennials continue to operate. It is common for artists to post something on one of their social media sites that will ultimately incite the intended target. Of course, the target can now instantly reply —and just like that—an internet beef has been spawned. It is usually the intent of the artist to start a beef; but sometimes an artist is just rapping and talking about no one particularly. It is the other artist's ego that causes him to believe that subliminal shots are being taken at him. In turn, he feels that he must defend himself and send shots back to the other artists. Sometimes the Millennial or Zoomer Era artist may throw a few shouts at an artist from the Foundational and Golden Era of rap. This has proved to be a mistake for these newer artists because the older artists from prior rap eras believed in physically seeing you about any beefs. These artists in the information age sometimes forget that life really exist outside the world wide web. They must learn that some men will follow through with their promises; and you might just get a fist to your face when we meet.

As technology compounds and proliferates daily, so does the ways the artists use it. Now artists can go live and share their lives in real time. Recently this new tool has gotten several artists into daunting situations with their rap peers and their fans. Posting something on social medial out of emotions can end up hurting the artist, or anyone for that matter. Most of the time, the artist is made to backtrack his or her statements when posting something before thinking about it. If the artist is big enough, a publicist and the record label would strongly encourage some sort of apology. Today the rap artist has become so comfortable speaking about their personal feelings in front of a camera, that they all come off as reality TV stars. I like to call this new phenomenon, "Reality TVism"! My conjecture is that today's artist has become too relax displaying their personal business for the world to see. Although I believe that most of reality television is scripted; I still do believe that the images portrayed are too personal. The rap artists who were raised on reality television is now mimicking what they grew up watching. The Zoomer Era rappers have it much worse than the Millennials; yet the current rap climate is still being ran by the Millennials, until further notice.

Rap beefs are now played out in front of the world on social media. Threats are sent at the speed of a finger pressing the send button to opposing emcees across the nation. Smart phones have made it much easier to reply to someone in real time. It is also more difficult to pretend that you did not hear what someone said about you because they are several gossip sites and wannabe online reporters breaking and spreading the news 24/7. It is to the point where information is literally old after a 48-hour cycle. Peer pressure will encourage someone to respond even if it is not in their nature to do so. The hip-hop rap arena is a blood sport that only the strong can ascend in. The time is gone where it was more respected to wait and talk to someone in person. We used to wait until we saw someone in person to ensure that what we thought we heard was true. Until then, everything else was consider hearsay, and we did not give our energy or time to it. The quick responses that we see today with this generation has caused men to gossip more about each other. If you don't respond to some rumor immediately, then the court of public opinion will deem you guilty. If men are to stay abreast to the ever-going information being produced; one must stay connected to social media or discuss it with their peers. Men are now talking on the phones about lives of other people who they do not even know outside the world of social media. It is turning men into "chatty patties" and making us more feminine in our communication with one another. Young black men have become more emotional, and one can assume that this is due to a lack of black fathers being in the homes to show them how to respond.

TRACK #20: BABY FACE GANGSTERS

T oday they are only a handful of mainstream artists who make conscious rap music with a strong message for the radio. To make it in rap you must be willing to do and say anything. It is now required to have zero inhibition and a miniscule amount of moral values for young rappers today. Think about a modern-day minstrel show being presented as reality, this is what the current rap game look like. This new rap business model brought in the rappers who could only articulate what they participated in, while in their own communities. They could only rap and appeal to those within their inner circle. These rappers have very little creativity in their rhymes. All it took was for one of them to sell a few records, then the flood gates opened for more just like them to ride the wave. The record labels, as per usual, began looking for copycat acts hoping to attain the success of similar successful acts. This could have been due to a shift in the creative control of the artist. The suburban kids were always enamored with the lives of the rappers in the videos; they strangely wanted to be able to identify with our struggle. It would not be long before these same observant suburban kids would learn about how the economics flowed in rap. Non-threatening rap acts began to incorporate gang culture in their music. White pop artists and non-gang related teens began doing gang related dances in their videos and in the clubs they attended. Yuppie white kids, who would usually follow the latest preppy trends, started to mimic the popular rap artists of the time. This new paradigm in the rap community slowly began to take the edge away from the music...at least in mainstream rap music. Now, A&R's and music executives began looking for artists with crossover appeal. White artists with street appeal and a certain look began being labeled as rap on the charts. Artist needed a hit song that would appeal to a broader audience. They needed a radio hit if they wanted to get any backing from their record labels. The rap artist who had signed record deals did not mind who were buying their records if the record was charting. This typically meant that more records were being sold.

The rappers from past rap eras had become too smart to sign the new 360 deals that labels were offering. To continue being profitable, record labels had to search for young starving artists to sign. Thus, you have young teens rapping about adult life situations none of them had ever experienced. In the Golden Era of rap, we had young rap artists who were guided by elder mentors. The music that was written for these kids still sounded like topics kids would discuss. The child rapper with pop appeal is now a thing of the past. These Zoomer Era kids now rap about sex, drugs, and murder straight out the gate. Young adolescent kids with face tats and drug addictions boast about their sexual escapades over heavy based musical tracks. In their defense, the Golden Era did have teenagers who made raps with adult subject matter; but the profanities were written in a way that was less overt. Still, many adults during those past eras did not like the rap music that was being played by their kids. The teens from the Foundational and Golden eras of rap were able to make music that is considered as classics today. Today the words are presented right in our faces with less creative wordplay. These kids are promoting very dangerous lives by celebrating drug use and collecting bodies on their records. Most of our GOATS of rap music have storied criminal backgrounds; if they were not the pusher, then they were the stickup kid or the street hustler. So, can we blame the young rappers of today for their subject matter? I can tell you this, most rappers from the past eras used their stories to show their humble beginnings and to establish a rags-to-riches storyline. Others use their past to separate themselves from those with less street credibility; and to establish their criteria for what would be considered authentic.

The current leaders of the rap game, Millennial Era rappers, rap about their struggles coming up in the streets or their affiliation with gangs. The smarter rappers make sure that it is known that the music is only a reflection of their real lives. Some of these rappers were true thespians before they started acting like gangster street rappers. So, it should be expected for these kids to come into the game with a scripted criminal background or storyline. Contrarily, the difference I noticed between the Millennial Era rappers and the current Zoomer Era rappers is that the later does not feel the need to pay homage to those that paved the way. They feel as if they do not owe the rappers from past eras nothing for their current success. I personally believe that these less than grateful Zoomer Era artists entered the rap game as opportunist to only gain financially; this is understandable. They could care less about the historical nature of the rap music industry; or about the rap titans who helped grow the culture to what it is today. Instead, they look at any form of critique as hate; or believe that the person critiquing them are too old to understand their music. I do believe that we sometimes age out of the subject matter being rapped about; but you are never too old to critique something you do not like. There are some exceptions who stand out from the pack of their Zoomer minded peers. These are usually the artist who study the past to help guide them into the future. These are the artist who are mentioned when one of the GOATS are asked, "Who do you currently like or listen to in the rap game?" The next time that question is asked to one of the GOATS, listen to the names they drop; these are the future greats of the game.

NEW AGE ELEMENT III:

Attention

TRACK #21: A NEW SKILL
RAP REQUIREMENT

Attention is the new currency! I have heard this sentiment echoed on several online and social media sites in this information age we currently live in. This statement deems to be true in several different ways. The first way I can say that this statement is true is that the more views a site receives, the higher the possible income it can generate. Advertisers pay money to those social media personalities with a huge following. Another way this statement deems to be true is that the more attention your site receives the higher the sale potential increases if you are selling a product or service. The more eyeballs your site receives, the higher the earning potential. Another way this is true is that the more followers you have automatically gives you a list of potential buyers of what you are selling through your site or page. These followers are all potential clients/buyers; and it makes it easier to reach out and advertise to them. The increased number of followers and views give each page or site owner the power to charge for higher advertisement fees, and to sell more of what they are selling.

The idea of attention being the new currency is not a concept that is limited to the current generation. Throughout the history of mankind, man has sought the attention of someone at some point in his life. The saying, "There's no such thing as bad publicity!" is a phrase that has been around since the early twentieth century. It implies that publicity of any kind should be looked at as a benefit to the person in question.

Many celebrities of the past have benefited from situations and incidents that most people would consider was done in poor taste. These situations have catapulted their careers into instant stardom. Others have become infamous; yet only remembered for the incident they were involved in. Still, some were able to parlay their publicity into a long-standing Hollywood career. Today, most famous people hire publicist to handle their public personas. The publicist job is simply to make the celebrity look good in the eye of the public. A good publicist can turn any bad situation into one that will benefit the client, or at least calm the waters enough to keep them working. In the world we live in today, a good publicist must be proactive and get ahead of a matter before the information is received by the public. If the court of public opinion receive the information before a publicist can react, it then becomes almost impossible to reverse their thinking.

As a youth many boys vied for the attention of a girl they fancied. We tried to accomplish this task by trying our best to impress the girl. Some guys attempted to be the best at everything. This included, marbles, spinning tops, black flips, football, basketball, etc. I mean we did our best to show the girl that we were the best. Other guys tried to wear the nicest and flyest clothes; or they always kept a fresh haircut. Still, some guys went as far as fighting and beating up the guy they thought the girl really liked in hopes that a victory would force her to like him. We did all of this just to get a little attention. Attention is a powerful drug, too much is dangerous!

TRACK #22: ORIGINAL ATTENTION SEEKERS

(Foundational Era)

I believe that the concept of seeking the attention of others have always been pervasive in the culture of rap music. The early participants of the culture understood the importance of seeking to earn the attention of the people. Most grew up in communities where certain individuals were lauded just for being the most popular person in the hood. The popular people in our communities were automatically appointed as the leaders in the neighborhoods. We cared about their thoughts and opinions, and we gave them the attention they were desperately seeking. The most popular kids in school also enjoyed the spoils of their popularity by being appointed in the leadership roles in the school's clubs and organizations. The hip-hop artist of the nineties grew up seeing how the most popular people in the community were treated. They noticed how easy it was for them to get the attention of the people. If you were lucky enough to grow up in a city that housed one of the founding fathers of hip-hop; you got a chance to witness how the people of the community watched their every move. Why did these individuals gain so much attention from their peers? How did they know what to do to earn the attention of others? What made them stand out from everyone else looking and hoping for the attention of others? As a youth we start out craving the attention of our parents. As we began to age, our need for attention pivots to that of our peers. We vie to earn the attention of the pretty girls in school; we fight for their attention. We try to excel and do well in school to get our parents attention; but if that doesn't work, we act out in school searching for the same outcome. As adults our crave for attention continues while in college and on the job. We are always competing to get attention from someone. We just want the attention to be considered the best at something...Anything!

Back then, artists did not have social media to help them garner up any attention on their own. Aspiring rappers had to gain notoriety by being the best emcee in their respective communities, and eventually the entire city. This was accomplished by going to different neighborhoods to battle other upcoming rappers; and by entering and winning as many talents shows as possible. Eventually, kids took notice of how the local rappers started gaining all the attention of the neighborhood and wanted a piece of the action. They noticed how the rappers wore the flyest clothes and jewelry. They noticed how all the young girls gravitated towards them. Many onlookers would try their hand at rapping just to lobby for some of that attention. For some it worked because they were able to skate by with minimal talent; but for the majority it failed. In the Golden Era of rap music, you truly had to have skills to make it in the game. Although ghostwriters were around then; it was still taboo to be known to have a ghostwriter. It was mostly CEOs-turned-rappers, who were given a pass for having a ghost writer, and maybe some rap music producers. Any other rapper in the business who was caught with a ghostwriter, was ostracized, and kicked out of the circle of true emcees. Biting another rapper was also considered sacrilegious; and was heavily scrutinized. Any rapper caught biting another rapper could have been exiled from the rap game permanently!

TRACK #23: A NEW TOOL
IN THE BUSINESS SHED

When rap music started, the act of rapping alone was enough to get the attention the rappers were looking to achieve. There was not a need for anything other than the words of the emcees to get the people's attention. Rap music was a new and refreshing artform that forced people to gravitate towards it. It was like witnessing a masterpiece for some; and like driving by a bad accident for others. Either way, people were paying attention to what was happening. As time would pass, and rap became more familiar, it needed a way to solidify its identity. Now that they had the people's attention, what would be the next move to keep it? How are we going to grow the artform? What will distinguish us from other forms of black entertainment? Rap music was almost at an impasse, and many pundits in the music industry had predicted that it would not continue to grow. It was said that rap music was a fad and should not be taken seriously. There were a few small labels who believed in the direction of the music; but this was well before the white corporate executives knew of its value. Rap music needed a way to keep its edge and the people's attention!

During the Foundational years of hip-hop, the artists knew that they had to wear a uniform on stage to separate them from the crowds coming to see them. They realized that the way an artist dressed played a major part in formulating the image they were trying to portray. To do this, they began dressing like the music artists who came to prominence before them. They wanted to look like the performing artists they grew up watching in the sixties and seventies. Back then, the artist wanted to stand out from the crowd. They wanted to people to look and gawk at their appearance, to be in awe of what they were seeing. In the seventies the large bands wore outfits that stood-out from the pack. They wore outlandish outfits that forced all eyeballs to pay attention to them while they performed. The rock bands, funk bands, and rhythm and blues bands all wore unique outfits on stage. The reasons the Foundational Era rap artists wore rock/funk influenced outfits was mainly due to rock artists being the only artists they saw on television and in magazines at the time. This was also true because they wanted hip-hop to be respected like the rock artists they watched on television. They wore outlandish outfits to separate themselves from their peer groups. The more bazaar the outfit, the more eyeballs were attracted to the performer. They wanted to look the part. The outfits became so over-the-top that they began to look like Halloween costumes on stage. During those Foundational years, the outfit was equally as important as the music. This was true for both individual acts and groups. The Foundational artists were seeking out the attention of the masses in hopes that someone would pay attention to their music. Once they were able to hook you with their clothes, the next goal was to get you hooked to their music.

The landscape would eventually change around the early eighties as rap music started to get nationwide notoriety. Acts started to dress like they would normally dress in the neighborhoods they came from. They went from wearing tight leather pants and tight shirts to looser fitting jeans and sneakers. The rappers wanted to dress like the drug dealers they saw in their communities. The drug dealers wore extravagant hood attire and lots of gold jewelry. They drove the flyest cars and wore the freshest clothes. The girls in the neighborhood fawned over the drug dealer's wardrobe and persona. They fantasized to be with the drug dealers. It was only natural for the rap artists to eventually gravitate towards the neighborhood superstars they grew up watching. In the mid-eighties the rap game witnessed a switch in the way the rap artists would dress. Of course, it was still ideal to be uniformed as a group; but the uniform had changed from tight polyester pants and blouses to tee shirts, jeans, and sneakers. As with most trends, this would spread throughout the rap community. Rap artists would now start dressing like the fly guys in their hoods whenever they performed. This included wearing the expensive jewelry and the most expensive clothes on the market. Many designer clothing labels owe rap artists for helping promote their brands to the black demographic. We wore the designer labels because our heroes wore them on stage and in their music videos. Most individuals would not be able properly pronounce some of the designer label brands if it were not for rap artist stating it in their music.

TRACK #24: EDUCATION?

I grew up wanting to be a lawyer, doctor, or a fireman! I was in the fifth grade and rap music had just became the music of choice for the youth in my community. This was the Foundational Era, and rappers were looked at like superheroes to many of us during that time. At that time, in the Dirty South, being a rapper was the last thing we thought we could be professionally. Although we knew it to be impossible, many of us still aspired to one day rap to make a living. A couple of my childhood friends didn't get this memo, and they were able to have some success as local kid rap celebrities. The rest of us realized that, only rappers in New York could make it for real. This notion was because most of the major record labels were headquartered in New York. Consequently, our only options were to be a fan of the music or hope that someone would send our music to a record label in the Big Apple.

By the time I reached sixth grade, rap music was the most important aspect in my life! I listened to tapes of my favorite rappers from the time I got up and headed out the door for school, to right before I closed my eyes for bed at night. I also began to realize that my family was poor, and we did not have the necessities needed to even survive in the ghetto. Being a realist at 11 years of age, I decided to switch my focus from being a rapper to becoming the smartest kid in school. My thinking back then was to get good grade so I can get an academic scholarship, become a lawyer, and buy my momma a house. Ironically, this was the thinking for most of the kids in the ghettos...the get rich and buy your momma a house part.

As I walked across the stage clutching my eighth-grade diploma, I shook my principal's hand for the last time in middle school. Before my summer ended, the paradigm had shifted when I entered high school. Somehow it became cool to not be smart, and now everyone wanted to be a rapper or an athlete. What changed you asked? Well, for those of us wanting to become rappers we learned that most of them had not been to college; and some of them had not finished high school. Yet, many of them seemed to be living a life of abundance and happiness. I understood that they had found a glitch in the matrix, a way to survive without having permission to. I knew that the rappers I listened to could have been anything they wanted to be, but rap was their profession of choice. Unfortunately for many of the youths growing up in the black ghettos of America, rap was considered an easy way out. These youths began to shun the idea of education, not realizing that to grow you must study your past. To be the best at anything you must study diligently. Do you believe that the current rappers have studied the history of rap?

The Western society have convinced us all that formal education is the only way to be successful here in America. The teachers tell their students that getting good grades will allow them to go to college. The college professors, in most HBCUs, teach that graduating from college is the only path to having a "good" job in life. Once we figured out how to acquire a bachelor's degree, the goal post is moved; and now you must have a master's degree to be successful. We go on to get the master's degree; but now you must have a Doctorate's, or the university is not accredited enough in the eyes of those who do the hiring. All a while, those of us who are not on an athletic or academic scholarship end up owing massive amounts in student loans. Only to get a job that does not pay you well enough to pay your loans back while simultaneously having a decent living. No one ever told us that we could earn a trade, skip the student loan debt, and still create a sustainable life for ourselves. No one ever mentioned the fact that most white-collar corporate jobs are based on cronyism and nepotism; and our chances of getting hired coming from an HBCU is null. So, being a post-college grad who have been through the trials and tribulations of working for small corporations, I fully understand why someone would choose to skip college and work for self. I envy those who were able to follow their passion and turn it into a thriving career. I use that envy for motivation; and truthfully, now that I understand, I am proud of them. It seems to me that the rappers knew something us college students failed to learn while going to school...You do the Math!

TRACK #25: FLY GUYS
(Golden Era)

As the Golden Era artist began to blossom, they also wanted to garner the same attention that the Foundational Era artists had gained. So, they too began to focus on their wardrobe. This is when the sneakers and jeans began to surface in the hip-hop community! But, just changing their wardrobe was not enough for these new rap artists! They wanted to do something that would identify them singerly from their Foundational contemporaries. Contrarily, although they loved the attention their wardrobe brought them; they still wanted to do more to separate themselves. To get the attention they so craved, the rap artist began to wear lots of jewelry—particularly gold rope chains with heavy medallions. The large gold necklaces were call "Truck Jewelry"! As large as the chain was, the medallion had to be just as large. Most of the jewelry the rappers wore back then were gold plated or just faux gold. But it was enough to give the Golden Era rappers in hip-hop the attention they were so desperately seeking! As time would pass through the eighties and nineties, the style of the jewelry would also change. Rap artist began to wear platinum instead of gold! The clothing got baggier … much baggier! Soon it became taboo to wear form fitting clothes; and the more oversized the clothes were, the more hip-hop you would look.

The Golden Era artists noticed the power and influence they had over the youth who looked up to them. They realized that these kids would mimic everything they did and wear anything that they wore. The large multi-national organizations also realized the marketing power the rap industry carried. They began to hire rap artists to promote and market their products. In the nineties you saw artists selling several different types of products. They sold everything from soda and clothing brands; and would eventually begin to sell alcohol brands as well. Consequently, they also sold a lifestyle to the impressionable youth that many of them were not actually living. The "shiny suit era" would also expound on the extravagant lifestyle many rappers portrayed. I too was a victim of the fakery that many of these artists displayed in their music and in their music videos. At one point, I felt that I had to really be in the streets to be a rapper. Little did I know that most of the successful rap acts were just that—Actors! This was way before the invent of social media. As a result, the fans did not have an inside view of what the artist' personal life was like. Therefore, the fan believed everything they saw the artist do on television or spoke about in their records.

Around this time, the corporations started to notice how lucrative the hip-hop rap music business had become. Rappers began signing to larger labels, and the labels began providing them with the necessary accoutrements most artist required under contract. This included, but was not limited to, access to the company's attorney; a publicist when needed; taking private flights across country to perform; and lodging in 5-star luxury hotels to party and bullshit afterwards. The rap industry had grown into one of the largest industries in the world. Rap music had made its way onto every continent, and the music was appreciated more by the new fans in these foreign countries. The Golden Era produced several of the hip-hop moguls we see in the rap game today. It introduced a decadence that had never been seen before in the rap industry. Themes like, 'Money, Hoes, and Clothes' became the mantra of the time. The cost of the jewelry increased and so did the number of vehicles. During the golden era, money became more important than getting the girl. This was mostly because, the more money you acquired, the more women you attracted. Therefore, consequently, these rappers had their choice of women. The Golden Era rappers no longer had to do extras to get the attention they were craving. Rap music was so popular at the time that the people outside the industry had to do things to get their attention.

TRACK #26: ONLINE STUNTIN

S ocial media has truly taken over the minds of the youth—and quite honestly—the masses! Not only had attention become the new currency; but it had people addicted to it like a new drug. Social media sites are the new business offices for those looking to earn some discretionary income. The individuals will stop at nothing to gain more followers with hopes that something of theirs will go viral. Most of the first viral online videos were that of people fighting! At some point during the outset of the social media craze; posting fight videos was a quick way to garner multiple views. The online social media paradigm quickly shifted from posting videos of cute pets to people fighting over nothing; or videos of women fighting over men. I would be remised if I did not shed light on the racial overtones of the videos being posted. Sure, I do not believe that there was some evil white man making people post certain videos; but I do believe that some sites encouraged it. Also, the mere fact that the videos were quickly going viral; would lead one to believe that the white viewing audience was also thoroughly enjoying these mockery type videos. It was like modern-day minstrel shows with black faces that did not need any painting.

Many of the social media viewers who helped these videos go viral were non-Black. They would show these videos to their peers and family members while lambasting our lifestyles and behavior behind closed doors. Yet, simultaneously, making black people the butt of the jokes they shared within their social circles of friends. It helped by continuing to spread the propaganda of blacks being uncivilized savages. These videos would also play a part in the desensitization of black people through the eyes of other ethnic groups. Other races stood by while innocent black people were being killed in the streets. Deep within their psyche these other races feel that the punishment is justified based on how we are objectified as untrained animals to the world. Yet, buried in their subconscious is the guilt of their relatives, and their entire race; of how poorly they have treated Africans in the United States. It also helped to encourage those ignorant black people, mostly the youth, to continue putting up like content.

Paradoxically, these same slanderous videos have been beneficial in decreasing the social gap wedged between black and white relations amongst Millennials and Zoomer aged kids. The youth of the current generation have decided that they would live in the present and not let the past transgressions of their parents define them. The online video did for the Millennial generation what hip-hop did for the generation before. It invited people from other cultures in to have a birds-eye view of how young black people were living in the ghettos of America. It helped to influence the way many of them would begin to carry themselves socially. It also helped incarnate black people in the mind of other races of people. Eventually, this would lead to other races mimicking the way the people acted and talked in the videos. Slowly you began to see other non-black ethnic groups using the word 'nigger' or 'nigga' when communicating amongst their peer group. Many of the Golden Era rappers took offense to allowing non-black ethnicities to use the word without any consequences. But the Millennials, and the Zoomers saw nothing wrong with these individuals using the word in their company. They even began to shun the Foundational and Golden Era rappers for making such a big deal about it. The online fighting videos looked like they could have been the motivation for the reality television we see today. The videos are big and polarizing; and look as if they are almost scripted and well thought out. How is it that so many people are readily prepared to record at the exact moment these incidents break out? It is truly becoming more difficult to know if a video is authentic or not.

The online video craze would continue to grow, and the creative minds of the world would follow! I.T. masterminds and tech geeks from around the globe began creating apps, and online sites, designed around social media. Armchair directors and wannabe be television stars quickly took advantage of these sites. A slew of internet comedians became stars from posting their videos on these sites. Some sites reacquainted old high school friends; and made it easier for faithful couples to cheat on one another. While other sites marketed infidelity as their focal point to direct internet traffic towards their website. Anyone with a camera phone could post videos of themselves doing something outlandish just to gain some views. It created a world where it was difficult to determine what was real or not. Shock videos became a genre within the social media video producing world. These shock videos were mostly staged performances of people doing just about anything for shock value and the attention of the unsuspecting audience. The performers would stage fake fights or outlandish behavior at the expense of surrounding people who had no idea about what was happening. Some performers would put their lives in danger just to pull off the most daring act they could legally get away with. Some of them would defy the laws of the land just to get a response. Some would go as far as committing suicide for attention. Nothing was off the board if it meant that they could possibly go viral. All of this was done for the sake of just getting some Attention! What a shame!

TRACK #27: I KEEPS IT REALITY
(The Millennial Era of Attention)

The millennials of today's rap industry are still striving for the attention required to become a rap star. Though there are some Millennial Era rappers who are considered the leaders of the rap game, many of them still are not household names. In fact, the rap industry has loss some of the attention it held during the Golden Era. The industry barriers-of-entry has lowered so much that anyone can now step over and enter the rap game. The hip-hop rap industry has become totally run by the corporations; and the smaller labels are huge A&R store fronts for the larger corporations. Today it is even more difficult to stand out from the crowd! This is mainly because the gatekeepers no longer hold all the control. It is also much easier to break into the rap game; but contrarily, it is even more difficult to become a star in the industry. Paradoxical as that may seem, the underground rap scene is inundated with hip-hop rap hopefuls looking to break through the crowd. The technology to record music improved with the maturation of the rap game. Computer software made it much easier for anyone to record their music and release it in the buyers' market. This, along with the invent of social media; opened the flood gates for any independent artist looking to be heard.

The Millennials are competing with the offspring of the Golden Era rappers. They are becoming the elders in the current rap game; and are being threatened to be pushed out by the Zoomers. These kids are even more tech savvy than their millennial older brothers. They are finding new and more inventive ways to have their music heard by the masses. The Millennials can feel the pressure of the younger generation like how the Golden Era rappers felt their presence and hunger for acceptance. Yet, the difference between how the Millennials entered the rap game and how the Zoomers are entering is respect! For the most part, the Millennials had respect for the Golden Era rappers and looked to earn their respect. Contrarily, the Zoomers are not asking nor looking for anyone's respect, they just want the drugs, fame, and money. The Zoomer Era of rappers could care less about culture or about the Foundational Era rappers who started the rap industry. They approach the rap game with a lassiez-faire attitude, and only care about their present state in the game.

When the Millennial Era rappers started entering the game, they were the offspring of the Foundational Era rappers. They are the babies of the rap stars from the 70s and 80s. Many of them were born during the Golden Era and had witnessed how huge rap had become. They wanted what they saw in the videos. The idea of having an abundance of money and having any woman you wanted drove them too push for more. The mainstream rappers of the Golden Era had laid the foundation for the future generations of the rap game. They touted and preached about Money, Clothes, and Hoes! This mantra was imbedded into the minds of the young future Millennial Era rappers who wanted to do things bigger and better. Consequently, the era of the millennial rappers emerged around the end of the 90s to the early 2000s. They were a few Golden Era aged rappers still making quality music and mainstream radio hits around this time. The Millennials had also witnessed how some of the Golden Era rappers had shunned the Foundational Era rap artists to make a name for themselves. The same Foundational Era artists who were the parents of these fresh-faced Millennials could have had an axe to grind; but they welcomed working with the old and new eras of music. Similarly, there were a few Foundational Era artists still making new music; but the majority had become extinct!

The Millennials would go on to carve out a niche for themselves! They were the first to fully shift the paradigm in rap by willingly seeking to work with other top rappers of their era. Many of them also reached back to work with their OG's of the Golden Era. They came of age just as social media began to take off. Some of the stars of their era were older in age, yet new to the rap game. Others were younger than the median age of the Millennial Era rap star. Several of the Millennial Era rap stars were born in the 80s. So, by the turn of the century, they were coming of age and leaving their adolescence. These new rap stars who gained some success in the early 2000's, still carried themselves like the stars of the Golden Era. But, all of that would slowly start to change around the middle of the decade. The abundance of money was not the same as it was during the Golden Era. Just like the generation before them; the Millennial Era rappers began looking for ways to stand out from their Golden Era contemporaries. Like the two prior eras, the change would start with their appearance. A person's appearance leaves a first impression and shows the world your personality and identity without you saying a word. This was around the time the Millennials would skip a generation and go back to how the Foundational Era rappers wore their clothes; but with their own added flava. It was the introduction to the skinny jean era. The younger Millennial Era rappers began to look at their rock star brethren for ideas to spice up their wardrobes. Just as the Foundational artists did in the beginning, so did the Millennials who were still searching for their own identity.

The Millennials needed a way to separate themselves from the Golden Era rappers who had basically brought rap into homes around the world. To do this, they had to come up with some self-identifying traits that would only be relatable to their generation of fans. As the jeans got skinnier, so did the rest of the wardrobe. Rappers now began to wear more form fitting clothes, similar to the Euro style of dress. It was almost as if they were telling the Golden Era rappers, "We can stand on our own!" This blatant change of the standard rapper's wardrobe almost instantly began to divide the fan bases of the two generations. The Golden Era rap fan was not too keen on the wardrobe changes in rap music. They looked at the new rap star as being "soft" or "corny" or need I say "gay" for wearing such tight fighting clothing. Contrarily, the Millennial rap fan rebutted and recanted and began calling the Golden Era rap fan "Old Heads" who were out of touch with modern fashion. Nevertheless, the way the Millennial Era rapper began to change the way he dressed instantly brought them the attention they had been craving. The Millennial Era rappers continued to search for more schemes that would bring them even more attention. The internet and social media were now easily accessible, and it was becoming more difficult to stand out from the regular non-rapping populace. In addition, technology had made it so that everybody and their momma was able to put out rap music. As I previously stated, the barriers of entry were low. So, the mainstream rappers needed something that would make them stand out and look the part. To add to their look, they decided to borrow even more from the punk rock culture by adorning their entire bodies with tattoos.

Caveat Interlude:

There is evidence of Egyptian women having tattoos as early as 4000 B.C. and men from other cultures dating back to similar times. As time would progress, the cultural acceptance of having tattoos would change from millennium to millennium. As a youth growing up in the early 80s, we were taught that people with tattoos were considered bad or dangerous. Guys would come home from prison covered in tattoos that they acquired while being locked up. We called them, "Jailhouse tats" because they were done while in jail, and you could tell they were not professionally done. These aspiring tattoo artists would come home and began practicing their craft on the kids in the neighborhood. Some of them were neophytes while others had been locked up long enough to perfect their craft. These self-made tattoo artists would build their own tattoo guns or just use a stick pin and Indian ink. The tattoos were usually just the initials

of loved ones or born date of a deceased relative. Most of these tats
would begin fading after a few years of sun exposure.

Rappers having tattoos was nothing new to the hip hop community; but facial tattoos were a little bit more extreme. Growing up in the eighties having a face tattoo meant one of two things: either you had killed someone in your past, or you were a part of a subculture or biker gang! Yet, the Millennial Era rappers decided that it would be a cool gesture to start tatting their faces. Besides, every other body part had already been covered. This attention-grabbing stunt was successful! It was enough to get the eyeballs it was intended to grab, yet too much for the armchair-wannabe rapper to commit to. Mainly, because most armchair-wannabe rappers were still working a 9 to 5 to support their rap dreams. Or, was too afraid to take a leap of faith to follow their dreams. So, when you saw someone with a face tattoo around that time in the streets; he was either a drug dealer trying to be a rapper or a wannabe rapper trying to portray a criminal past.

In addition to the facial tattoos, I would be remiss if I did not mention that the Millennial Era of rap brought in the idea that you had to come from a criminal background in order to be consider a gangster rapper. During this era, it became a requisite to really come from the streets or poverty if you wanted to be taken seriously. Suburban kids with really good writing skills could not attempt to come out during this era without a street cosign. This ushered in the real street 'goons' to play a vital role in the rap game. The new mainstream rappers coming out in this era either sold drugs or was a part of some type of criminal culture. Or they paid some real street goons for protection and street cred. In fact, a few of the biggest rap stars of the era were former drug kingpins (most self-proclaimed) who were given an opportunity by a record label. Many of them claim to have already acquired wealth and street fame before entering the rap game. They wore their past criminal proclivities like a badge of honor. Contrarily, the writing skills of the music would begin to decline; and rappers with exceptional writing talent would be overlooked for image. The Millennials brought in the rappers who boasted, or really could care less, about their lack of intricate rhyme patterns and metaphors. These rappers coin themselves as "Game Spitters"; which basically meant that they only had to speak their reality! This type of creative ideology stifled creative lyrical growth! Thus, the influx of criminal wannabe rappers would begin the decline of quality music getting airtime on the radio. Unfortunately, the next era of rappers, The Zoomers, would grow up listening to the watered-down version rap on the radio.

TRACK #28: LOOK AT ME
(Zoomer Era Attention)

The generation following the Millennials are called Generation Z or Zoomers as they have been affectionately coined by some. This is the current era of hip-hop rap music, and they are the offspring of the Golden Era and some of the Millennials. The Zoomer Era blossomed into an era that was designed around getting attention. The Zoomers were born into the age of information and social media madness! It had witnessed some of the Millennial Era rappers become stars from posting their music on social media sites and blowing up. Social media has been a gift because of how easy it is to participate, and a curse for the same reason. As a result, social media had made stars out of people with little-to-no artistic ability; but they were equipped with strong will and drive. Contrarily, the talented ones who use social media to get discovered are now mainstays in our pop culture. The biggest social media stars got famous by clout chasing. The Zoomers learned this method of getting attention from some of the Millennial Era rappers before them. Clout Chasers get famous by attacking those who are already famous to get their attention. Any type of attention from the targeted famous person is a win for the Clout Chaser. And, like most mediums of entertainment that flourishes fame; copycat acts will soon follow the same blueprint. Thus, most of the Zoomer Era rappers came into the rap game with a clout chasing mentality.

The Zoomers would pick up where the millennials had left off! Many entrepreneurial zealots quickly took notice of people willing to showcase their lives on camera for attention. The local rap stars from around the country would start-out putting their material up on these sites designed to showcase the train wreck. Then the strippers, wannabe strippers, and porn stars followed by putting up their "advertisements" next. The industry took notice; and would start breaking their new rap artists on many of these sites. The first thing we noticed from the Zoomer Era rappers were the number of tattoos many of them sported coming into the rap game! They wore face tats like permanent jewelry! Every new "LiL" rapper was fully tatted by the time we realized who they were. Rappers, who were still in their teens, came into the rap game with permanent facial tattoos. It was if they lived by a 'make it in the rap industry or bust' mantra! One could only imagine how little control their parents had over their lives. This change in how kids are living like they are parentless could be attributed to several reasons. Particularly, black boys growing up in crime ridden cities by single black mothers. Consequently, most absentee black fathers are missing due to circumstances out of their control, i.e. school-to-prison pipeline, and white society's faux ignorance of black culture. But I digress because this is not about race.

In continuing with the tradition of the eras before them, the Zoomers also felt a need to create their own identity! And like those before them, this would lead to them altering the required uniform of a rapper. At some point towards the end of the Millennial Era, many rappers began having a deep interest into the rock star culture. Sure, most historians know that rock-and-roll started out as a culturally black music; but it does not sound like the rock music we hear today. Currently, rock music is known as a white music genre culturally! I am certain that the Millennial Era rap artists were not thinking about the forefathers of rock-and-roll when they decided to start imitating the culture. This theory could be proven by the rock artists the Millennial rap artists chose to mimic. Those rock artists were mostly popular white rock stars from the seventies and eighties. Some older white rock acts are even lauded by the Millennial and now Zoomer Era rappers. The infatuation seemed to be mostly with the image and lifestyle of these rock artists. Particularly, the clothes and the "Sex, Drugs, and Rock-and-roll" mantra was chosen as the attributes the Millennial and Zoomer Era rappers decided to follow.

The rappers of today are now being seen wearing tee shirts with old rock bands on them. They wear ripped skinny jeans, black fingernail polish, and ripped tees that resemble female blouses. Having an androgynous look is now avant-garde within the Zoomer Era rap culture. To speak out against the way these young male rappers are dressing could get that person labeled as being homophobic. Currently, at the time this book is being written, the LBGTQ community is very powerful in the world of entertainment. Where in the past it would have been a death sentence for a rapper to say anything remotely seen as gay; today it is almost applauded. But I digress! The Zoomer Era rappers could also be recognized for wearing extravagant and expensive designer brands that are known for not creating fashion for the "urban" demographic. Yet, the Zoomer Era rappers are aware that wearing certain designer labels resemble wealth; and they want to portray that image to their fans. The Zoomers have decided that they are "Doing Them" and could truly care less whether it is considered hip-hop or not. As a rap artist from the South, I can empathize with their struggle to be accepted by the rap Foundational Era rappers from the East coast; but I cannot accept them not paying homage to the forefathers of the rap game. Just to be different, many of the Zoomers have blatantly disrespected the artists that came before them. One could easily believe that the Zoomer rap fan must share the same sentiment for the artist to be so bold in their stance.

TRACK #29: THE INVISIBLE MEN

Mental illness has always been a taboo subject in the African American community. I can personally attest to many individuals walking the streets in my community whose mental instability went undiagnosed for years. The ghettos of New Orleans, in the 80s and 90s, were inundated with mentally ill individuals. Many of them were born to parents who used crack, nicotine, and alcohol when they were conceived. Their chances of success in this world was stifled from birth. These kids were the first victims of the crack era. They were the true "Crack Babies" who were born into chaos and self-destruction. They were not diagnosed with a mental disease because their parents lack the means to obtain the adequate medical attention they needed. In addition, admitting and accepting that a loved one was mentally ill was still taboo; and most people were too shameful. These kids grew up being ridiculed because they did not act like the other kids in class or in the neighborhood. Unless a kid was born with a physical deformity, it was highly likely that their mental problems were ignored.

These kids walked around looking normal; but they were suffering inside from thoughts they could not control. In most cases the mental deformity was so minor that any good therapist could have provided tools to help them cope. Instead, these kids would go through life trying to find a way to fit in with their peers. These were the kids who were easily influenced by any fad that took place in pop culture. They were the kids who always seem to get into some type of trouble at school. I personally used to wonder why some of the children could not stay out of trouble. Yet, these same kids were smart enough to mimic what they thought was cool. They would emulate the cool guys in the neighborhood who attracted all the attention of the girls in the hood. They wanted to be just like the guys who wore designer clothes and drove nice cars. They had no inner filter to control how they acted or what they did. These mentally challenged kids walked the streets like ticking time bombs waiting to be ignited. These kids were part of the beginning of "Attention" being the new currency. Getting the attention, they sought from their peers was enough to get them through their day. When the attention was not enough to satisfy their ego, they were willing to do whatever it took to quench it. They would become the yes men or the shooters for those they were looking to impress. They would go on dangerous missions, aka Dummy Missions, to secure the acceptance of the people they wanted to be like. The few of them who were able to acquire some material gain through selling drugs, were easily provoked and willing to literally kill any competition.

As I have gotten older and lived in several different cities around the country; I noticed that my upbringing in my hood was not unique. Nor was it limited to one ethnic group or another. If you grew up in an environment like mine, then you know of these people. Either you personally knew them, or you heard about them through word-of-mouth or because of their infamy. Today these would be the guys making the shock videos for attention, or the ones running inside convenient stores and gas stations shouting out profanities and intentionally causing a scene for the attention. What is even worse is that some of these guys became successful internet personalities and gained fans who valued their opinions. These are usually the black rappers/ entertainers that news organizations come to for their opinions about political and racial subjects. They usually voice an opinion that is not in unison with their core fan base; and then the fans accused them of being out of touch with certain topics. In their defense, I reckoned that there is some form of mental instability existing that has not been diagnosed. If the rapper is a cash cow, why would his handlers change anything to better him personally. In recent history we have seen rappers check themselves into mental health facilities to deal with the trials of everyday life. We have also seen, so called gangster rappers, turn witness to get themselves out of prison. One may argue that ratting on someone to better your own situation is a sign of natural intelligence. But I do not question the ratting part as being a sign of mental illness, I question the part that built this façade of creating a gangster image to boost his career.

I was recently scrolling through my social media and I stopped and watched a video someone put up about the protests currently taking place around the world. Like most of these videos, I knew it would be something showing in the video that would be polarizing. Most of these videos are usually one minute or less; but this one ran for almost two. In the video there was a young black woman, provocatively dressed, twerking in front a line of cops with riot gear on. This woman was shaking and gyrating on the ground, doing splits, and bending over for all officers, and the world, to see. The video became viral and the young woman got a lot of backlash from the court of public opinion. Of course, she mentioned that it was done to help shed light on the cause, and not herself. In the comments below the video, most people thought that it was done in poor taste; while some defended her actions as her doing what she could do to help. I personally believe that it was done in poor taste and that the young woman did it to only bring attention to herself. I think that she knew that the video would go viral; and that was her intent.

Attention Whoring is nothing new to the rap community! I define attention whoring as basically prostituting yourself to gain attention from an intended audience. Attention Whoring is not limited to only women, a lot of men also do whorish things online to gain some attention. During the Golden Era of rap, the female rappers started to gain some traction in the rap arena. These women were very talented lyrically; but did not receive the same amount of attention as their male counterparts. To gain the attention these female rappers craved, a couple of the top female rappers began dressing very provocatively in their music videos and promo posters. They also began centering their raps around their sexuality, and thus changed the narrative from being about lyrics to now being more about their look. I personally believe that this was a negative blow to the female rap collective. Future female rap aspirants now had to, not only focus on creating the best rhymes; but dress like hookers to get the attention they needed. Today women are doing any and everything online to get attention. Some women ridicule other women to make themselves more of a catch for the opposite sex. These women are called "Pick-Me's" meaning, to not pick her; but, pick me. Or, you may see women marching in the protest dressed scantily pretending that they did not notice that their ass was hanging out the back of their jeans. Female rappers today are still making overly sexualized videos. Unfortunately for them, this is the only lane they have to bring attention to their genre. Sex sells and these artists are doing what they need to do to compete with their male counterparts. We all have seen the disparity in pay when we compare women sports to men. These female rappers have found a way to get the attention they need to even the playing field.

The men are no different when it comes to showing their asses for attention. Guys would appear online shirtless, wearing gray joggers without underwear, talking about eating a proper diet. The idea is to pretend that they are only showing off their bodies to motivate others to do the same, but they are only doing it to get attention from females. Or you may see guys and girls doing workout videos to attract the opposite sex. Men are also simping at an all-time high in the Zoomer Era of music. Young men are putting up videos of themselves doing over-the-top prom proposals asking young woman to go with them to their prom. Or, men are supporting the social media attention whores by paying to view the adult material they put up for purchase. The game has truly changed, and young people are doing-the-most to get attention these days!

Caveat Interlude:

During the Golden Era of rap, a few rap stars became famous after surviving attempts on their lives. One of the most notable artists of the Golden Era survived several deadly shots and went on to make a couple of iconic rap albums afterwards. The Millennial Era would see another artist get shot multiple times, survive, and become more famous afterwards. This artist would also create his most notable work after surviving an attempt on his life. The rap aspirants noticed a pattern to skyrocket themselves to stardom. In the rumor mill I started hearing stories of lesser known artists having someone to intentionally shoot them so that they could become more famous. For most, this concept did not bear any fruit because what they failed to identify was that the artists before them had already gained a fanbase and some notoriety. They did not come from obscurity, get shot, then blow up in the rap game. This attention seeking concept became so ludicrous that is was mocked by comedians and in the movies.

NEW AGE ELEMENT IV: POPULARITY

We take a deeper look at who and what was popping during each era of rap.

TRACK #30: THE IN VOGUE IS KING

(The Foundational Era)

I n each era of rap music creation there has always been those involved who held positions that was most coveted by onlookers outside of the industry. These people would be considered the movers and shakers of the rap industry. These were the individuals that the fans and wannabes wanted to be like. These were the people that girls fawned over; and the men that women wanted to be with sexually. They moved the needle in the rap sales industry! They created the trends! They started and ended fads! They were the muses for the popular kids in the neighborhood! These were the people that everyone wanted to be like. They were the "Chosen" ones!

Throughout the history of hip-hop culture there was always an element that was more popular than others. The early 80s witnessed the graffiti artists and the break dancers be the most popular elements of hip-hop. Then the parties in the parks of New York saw the DJ emerge as the most popular. As time would pass, they all would give ground to the Masters of Ceremony aka emcee ka MC. The rapper would become the face of hip-hop, and it helped spread the culture around the globe. If hip-hop was a nation, the rappers became its ambassadors by representing the culture everywhere they performed. From the origins of rap up to the current Zoomer Era, there have always been trending fads that helped move the culture. Rap music itself was once a fad that has stood the test of time. It is the perennial element of the hip-hop culture, and it remains a favorite amongst the youth.

In the beginning of rap, it was the voice of the Disc Jockey (DJ) being heard over the break beats that ultimately created rap as we know it today. The DJ used his voice, and personality, to keep the crowd's attention as he searched through his crates for a new record to spin. The DJ also would be the voice of the establishment he was spinning for. He advertised upcoming events for the establishment; and helped the bartenders sell drinks to the patrons. The DJ held a position with very high barriers of entry due to the cost to buy the equipment; and the limited number of paying gigs. Most kids growing up during the beginning of rap wanted to be the DJ.

As rap music began to take off and become popular amongst the youth; the DJ had become a mandatory staple in the game. Neighboring crews would each have their own DJ who represented their hood. These DJ's would battle for supremacy to be known as the best in their city. They earned the support of their communities; and was placed on a pedestal that was difficult to reach by any aspiring up-and-comers! This was a time when the youth were trying to get over the blaxploitation era of the 70s. As the 80s rolled in, the black youths were searching for an identity of their own. They wanted to be a part of something that would define them and give them identity. They wanted to bring the fictional black superhero types they saw in the blaxploitation films to life! The hip-hop DJ's would become the, larger-than-life, figures that the black youths would lift-up to superhero status!

The catalyst of rap as we know it today was the disc jockey. As a kid growing up during the Foundation rap era; I could remember how the DJ held all the juice in the local music seen. If you wanted to throw a party, you had to— Hire a DJ! If you wanted to request your favorite record on the radio, you had to—call up the DJ! If you were throwing a block party, you had to—hire a DJ! If you opened a night spot, you had to—Hire A DJ! If you were running a strip club, you had to—Hire A DJ! If you went to a club and was looking for who was "holding something", you had to—Go See The DJ! The DJ was truly the man back in the early eighties. He had all the ladies; and he truly was responsible for the night life in your city! The DJ's prominence was a carryover from the Disco era of the 70s; consequently, many of the first DJs in rap music started out in the Disco clubs. Nevertheless, the DJ was the most popular figure in the hood during the Foundational Era of rap. If rap were a building, the DJ would be its foundation!

TRACK #31: MEDIUM EVOLUTION

T hroughout the rap eras, the way we listen to music has changed as the music aged. I believe that there is a positive correlation with our lifestyle and how we listened to our music. In the 60s and 70s people usually entertained themselves at home. As time would pass, individuals became more active, and the way we listened to music had to keep up. Before rap music was mainstream and I was still a little tike; I remember my elders playing their music on 12-inch vinyl LPs (Long Playing) and 7-inch vinyl called 45s for the RPMs. If you were born during the Foundational Era of rap, and you remember your parents playing music in the house, I can almost guarantee it was being played on vinyl records. They were two vinyl types at the time because competing record companies put out their own versions of vinyl records. These vinyl records had been around well before rap music was birthed and they were the main way our parents listened to music back then. Around the time I became aware of music in the 80s, there was another medium being used by individuals at home. This was the 8-track tape that became more popular than vinyl records because automobile makers started putting 8-track players in their cars. The 8-track tape resembled a video game cartridge in that the case was squared shaped and plastic. My childhood was filled with the sounds of all the old blues and jazz artists from back in the day. My grandmother's living room housed a rectangular 2'x 5'wooden 8-track and vinyl record player with large built-in speakers. The top was able to raise up and down; and on the inside there was space to hold your records and 8-track cartridges. The rectangular box looked like an antique piece of furniture. The house parties were smoked filled and the libations were that of beer and some type of whiskey. It was truly a vibe!

As our lives became more active and on-the-go, the way we listened to music had to keep up with our lifestyle. The 8-track cassette was minimized into a compact cassette that was much smaller and easier to carry around. Technology companies began making portable music devices to play the cassettes on. We would pop in our cassette and plug in the headphones and listen to the latest rap star on-the-go. The cassette would be our music medium of choice from around 1983 to 1991. In 1991, the compact disc would surpass the compact cassette and the music medium of choice would change once again. The compact disc or CD, as it is usually referred as, became the new way to listen to our favorite rappers. The technology companies quickly began to make portable compact disc players to keep up with the everchanging technology. Like the older mediums before, eventually companies stopped making compact cassette tapes. The compact disc would reign supreme for about ten years before another medium took over.

As we got closer to the year 2000 or 2k, our lives were becoming more digitized. Almost everything we did could be done using a computer. As we got closer to the end of the 20th century, we were dealing with conspiracy theories like the world coming to an end and Y2K. During this time, rap artists are still doing platinum record sales. Rap fans were still rushing to the record stores on Tuesday to see what new music was being released. Around 1999 there was some smoke surrounding a new way to consume music. The Millennials found a way to copy or rip music from another CD for free. The purchased CD's music would be uploaded to a file on a computer and then downloaded to an empty recordable disc. The download would take a very long time and was of poor quality, but ultimately the buyer of the copied CD would save money instead purchasing a new CD from the record store. Then the MP3 files were created, thus allowing the user to download a massive amount of material, with quality sound, at a much faster rate. This phenomenon birthed the "bootleg CD" hustle. This is when you could buy burned CDs for $5 or less from the neighborhood "Bootleg Man" seller. Next, a new online site was created that allowed users to share downloaded music files for free with users from around the globe. By this time, the sale of tangible CDs had severely declined. In 2001, a computer company would create a huge buzz around a portable MP3 player; and the CD sales world would come to a screeching halt.

Today the Zoomers no longer need MP3 players to listen to their favorite artist. You no longer had to download music to any type of file anymore to listen to your favorite artist. Around the same time the MP3 player was eclipsing the sales of CDs, another company unveiled a new way of listening to music called "Streaming". This new medium made it to where you no longer needed a device to download your music to, you could just visit the site or the app and press play. Well, you still do need some type of device to stream music; but you do not have to buy anything additional. Of course, as time would pass more companies presented more sophisticated ways to listen to the music. Streaming service companies would eventually put the MP3 devices to rest. Artists do make a little money every time their music is streamed multiple times. This concept is better than their music being pirated for nothing, but far less than they were making on the sale of a CD.

It is strange that every time a new medium was born, the older one had to die. It was as if no two mediums could coexist at the same time. Some may argue that as the technology got better there was no need for the older version. Others may say that, just because something is newer does not necessarily mean that it is better. I still have CDs that I listen to; I have too much in my collection to just stop. I also stream music and listen to downloads by playing them through my Bluetooth in my car.

The technology has also changed a lot for those looking to become a DJ in today's rap game. You can now become a DJ with a laptop and some speakers, shoot, you can buy digital turntables and make scratching sounds like vinyl records. Yet, if you ask a real DJ, if you know one, what they prefer, most will say spinning real vinyl LPs. So, does that mean that vinyl LPs are better than the current new technology, or is it just a matter of preference?

TRACK #32: NO, I'M THE RAPPER!

(The Golden Era)

As the DJ became the face of the hip-hop rap movement, his role in the game became bigger and bigger! As the money begun to pile up, so did the number of jobs. The popular DJs would hire other DJs to fill in for them when they could not make a gig. They would eventually formulate DJ crews, and thus was able to send out a multitude of DJs who represented the crew to different locations while still operating under the crew's name. To keep the crowds moving, the DJs would normally speak between records as to not change the mood of the room. Eventually, the DJ would hire someone to MC for him as he spun the records. This Masters of Ceremony would not only speak to keep the crowd involved, he also began to add clever rhyme patterns to his performance. This would be the beginning of the emcee/rapper we now know of today.

As rap music began to formulate and groups started to come together; small record labels would seize the opportunity to sign them. The DJ still had a major influence in the hip-hop arena; consequently, many of the signed groups were fronted by their DJ. You would see groups with the DJ's name first featuring a group of emcees. Or a two-man group where the DJ was the marquee and the emcee was in the background. This would continue well into the beginning of the Golden Era of rap! Then suddenly things began to change! When the groups would perform, the DJ would be in the background and the rapper would be at the front of the stage wooing the audience. This naturally evolved as the DJ's equipment was usually held behind the emcee. The people would come to the shows with antsy anticipation of hearing the voices they heard booming on records and through the radio. The pendulum began to swing in the opposite direction. The DJ, though still very much a necessary ingredient, had become the side dish to the emcee's entrée.

The Golden Era was the spawn of the true definition of what it meant to be an emcee. This was when labels began putting out records with the images of the artists on the album covers. For a while, when these albums were first released, and the public started to put faces to the names; many people thought the emcee was the DJ, and vice versa. This was because the DJ's name was usually placed first on the records. So, it was quite natural for the public to assume that the voice behind the music was the leader of the group. The concept of the person responsible for the music or the one responsible for putting the group together, but not being the front man, was not new to the music industry. Many of the rhythm-and-blues groups from the sixties and seventies had leaders who were not the lead vocalist or singer; yet, their names were first on the marquee. The name of the group was usually the founder's name first and then the group's name. For example: Terry Johnson and the Quarter Notes or The Quarter Notes featuring Terry Johnson. Either way, in most of those older bands, the leaders were not the lead vocalist or singer. This trend would continue in the rap industry. As I stated above, many DJ's started rap groups; and rightfully, they wanted to be recognized as the leader. Once the fans realized who was doing the rapping, the rapper automatically became the most popular of the group. The younger rap fans wanted to be like the rapper and not the DJ. The Golden Era most def belonged to the emcee. The era also saw the rise of the solo emcee who only needed the DJ to spin the records for him. The solo artist would blossom into the OG rap stars we know of today. Simultaneously, many DJ's would begin to take on the role of the music producer to continue having an imprint in the game.

TRACK #33: THE DJ STRIKES BACK
(The Millennial Era)

The Golden Era of rap saw the emcee take center stage as the most popular entity of the culture. Almost running concurrently was that of the music producer. Throughout the history of rap music there have always been a few DJs who were also very good music producers. Some of these DJs would produce and rap on their records, while others just spun and produced the records. Others were just given producer credits because they were a part of the group and Deejayed, but they really did not create the beat. Still these DJs would find a resurgence to play a very vital part in the hit making process. Towards the end of the Golden Era of rap, going into the Millennial Era, music producers became the main cog in making a successful rap record. This was when rappers had to have certain producers to help sell the album.

During the Golden Era of rap music there were a handful of excellent producers creating the soundscapes for the rappers to create masterpieces on. Some crews had their own in-house producer, while other artists had their go-to producers. The super producers only worked with the top selling artists at that time, while the lesser known producers were relegated to work with lesser known artists. Yet, many of the classic albums of that time did not focus around who produced the songs. If you think of some of the biggest hits from that time, except those put out by a super producer, you cannot think of who produced the record. Of course, in hindsight, many rap pundits may know now; but during the height of the record we only knew who the rapper was. This concept started to change during the Golden Era of rap music. The name of the producer became just as important as who was rapping on the track. Super producers had the power to catapult someone's career into one of fame and fortune. This power to elevate one's career came with a hefty price tag. The cost to get certain producers on a record could eat up half of a rapper's budget with the record label. To sell the record in interviews, the rapper would mention who the producers were on the record. As fans of rap music, we fell for the necessity of having a well-known producer on a record before we bought it. I reckoned that many good albums fell through the cracks because they did not have one of these producers.

Simultaneously, DJs were putting out mixtapes with rappers spitting over beats, and their names were the marquee. DJs putting out mixtapes were nothing new; but now they were releasing CDs under major labels. As the Millennial Era came into existence, you started to hear producers shouting out their names at the beginning of the record. Thus, the producer would be heard before the listener knew who would be rapping on the track. This "self-promoting" thing became infectious because all up-and-coming producers felt the need to shout out their names at the beginning of the record. We started to hear Joe Blows utilizing this tactic to become famous. I can say that for some, it worked, because some of the newer producers today got their start by doing this. The idea is to get a superstar rapper to use one of the tracks, this is usually done pro bono, to advertise their beat making skills to others. If Lil So-And-So uses the track and it becomes a hit, or if it is known that it was used by said artist; then the concept was a success.

Today the producer is equally as important as the rapper. The money they made during their height may have diminished a tad because there is less money, overall, in the rap industry. The top producers are the ones who are most requested by rap artists. This can only be because of their hard work and diligence to remain relevant in the rap game. Now it is customary to search for the producer of each track when a new album is released. This was not as important during the Foundational Era of rap. The change could just be a natural progression as rap began to mature. Producers are now releasing full-length albums featuring only one artist. These partnerships have generated some of the best albums of certain artist's catalogues. As fans, we have followed certain producers so closely that we know their sound as soon as the needle drop. We all have our favorite producer to listen to. I have mine! Who is yours?

TRACK# 34: A CHANGING OF THE GUARD

The OG Southern emcees started out rapping by putting their own spin on the music that came from the East and West coast. Southern rappers had a plethora of different styles that was comparable and even better than some of their East and West coast brethren. From the South came different rhyme cadences and patterns that had not been heard before on hip-hop tracks. With most of the Southern artists having some roots in the black church, you could hear the influence in the music. As the Southern emcee emerged, so did the Southern music producers. These Southern producers would begin to add their own flava to the music they produced. It was a base heavy sound that resonated with the core Southern rap fan. Each state in the South would produce a specific sound. The producers in Florida would create a sound for the clubs that was different in other Southern domains such as Houston or New Orleans. The drum patterns that the producer created provoked the women to dance provocatively on the dance floor. The women would gyrate their bodies in a very sexual manner and move their asses up and down to the beat of the music.

The provocative dances the women did with their asses was coined "pussy popping" in the South. I would like to think the term starting down in Miami during the 80s. The girls would use this as a quasi-mating call to attract the, more than willing, men on the dance floor. The producers in Texas would provide the landscape for a more gangster sound. The artists coming from the Texas label imprints would take us down a more sinister path. The beats were much slower, and the rap songs were more detailed and story oriented. The next Southern state that would emerge on the national rap scene was Louisiana. The producers provided a combination of the Florida booty shake music and the Texas slowed down gangster style. The rap artists would combine gangster styled lyrics over a booty shake beat. The artists, particularly in New Orleans, would create an up-tempo style of rap called Bounce Rap. The original bounce rappers all rapped about tales of criminal activity and promiscuous women. This would eventually lead to other styles of gangster rap emerging from the city. As a lifelong resident, I know that the influence of the music was due to the overly saturated crime element of the city. In the 80s and 90s, the city was inundated with criminals on both sides of the law. Therefore, the rap artists were able to give a first account of what was happening in the inner cities throughout the state. Simultaneously, the state of Georgia was making the most noise nationally. The city of Atlanta had become its own version of black Hollywood for entertainers. They would go on to produce some of the most successful rap artists, regardless of the coast, on the national stage the rap game has ever seen. By the turn of the twentieth century, Southern rap had become a mainstay in hip-hop culture.

Caveat Interlude:

To any hip-hop rap fan born in the nineties, you may look at the current rap climate like it has always been this way. The truth is, before the mid-nineties and up until now, there has been a bias against Southern rappers in hip-hop. I've been in chat rooms that discussed the top 10 rappers in the game and the Southern emcees are rarely ever listed. Even the Southern rapper(s) who are considered GOATS by their fanbases, are heavily scrutinized by the fans of West and especially East rappers. Even when the rappers themselves say that a certain Southern rapper belong in the GOAT conversation, there is still push back from the other coast fans. I am certain this is due to the stereotype of Southern people being mentally slower than people from other regions. Mind you, most blacks migrated from the South to states up North to find better job opportunities. Most blacks living in non-Southern states have family members who still live in the South. Or, it could be that we all just sound different. Either way, we always felt like we were being left out when people talked about the best rappers in the game. Contrarily, the South has had the longest run in the rap game thus far. The South always had something to say!

TRACK #35: PHONE GAME

From the beginning of time, man has always found a way to communicate with one another. Whether it was the beating of African drums, or the smoke signals of the Native Americans, communication was a necessity. My earliest recollection of communication was in elementary school. We would write notes and pass them to one another so we could communicate a message while class was in session. The note was usually the question we all were too afraid to ask in person: Do you like me, check Yes box or the No box. Waiting on the answer to get the note passed back was stressful and intense. There was always one knucklehead kid who wanted to read the note before passing it back to the person who wrote it. He would be the one the teacher would catch, and then get called up to read the note in front of the class. I never knew why the teacher punished the kid by embarrassing him until, well, until now. I guess it was the easiest way to prevent other kids from passing notes around in the future. We would also communicate by word-of-mouth, somehow the entire school knew who was going to be fighting once the school bell rang at 3:15.

As a boy growing up in the early 80s, I remember having a plastic mauve colored rotary dial phone with the long coiled curly cord connecting the handset to the base of the phone. The phone was usually housed in the living room and only adults could answer it. Using this phone in the living room left little room for any privacy or secrecy if you had someone special to talk to. Eventually, someone would make the long phone cords and the curly cords that connected to the phone. This allowed you to take the phone through the house and to your room to talk to your girl; but you still bet not had answered that phone first. The Golden Era of rap began, and the cordless house phone became available for the public to buy. The cordless phone made it much easier to maneuver around the house to find the privacy you needed; but you still bet not had answered your momma's phone before she did. At some point your parents started trusting you to answer the phone; and then the yells went from, "You bet not answer that phone!" or "Didn't I tell you not to answer the phone?" to "Boy, answer the damn phone, don't you hear it ringing?!". I know, confusing right; but there were several reasons you could not answer the phone as a child, as you got older you learned how to handle those calls.

Caveat Interlude:
*Before the cordless phones with the open message boxes hit the market, it was very difficult to screen calls. If a bill collector or someone you did not want to talk to would call, you had to answer the phone first to know who was calling. This made it very difficult to screen calls; thus, this was the main reason why parents did not want children answering the phone. Then we learned about dialing Star 69 or *69 on the phone which allowed you to listen to the last number and name of the registered user of the last call. Then people started using Star 67 or *67 on the phone to block the identity of the call. The Star 67 numbers would show up as private, and we never ever answered a private number. Your ex-girlfriend would try getting through with a Star 67 number; but we knew it was them who were calling. Once the cordless phones came out with the caller ID information screens, we were able to see who was calling before we answered. Or they still used the Star 67, and the message would say that it was from a private number; those got the same treatment as before.*

The Golden Era of rap was the height of drug dealing in the hood. Back then, the drug dealers used beepers to communicate with their customers. Rappers started talking about beepers in their music and they also wore them in the videos. It took no time for beepers to become a must have, and eventually every kid in the hood had to have one. Like house phones, the beepers also went through an evolutionary time span. The first beepers only allowed you to receive messages numerically. The beeper would beep, you would check the number, then you would go to the nearest pay phone to call them back. Imagine having to keep several quarters on your person to call back the number. We got clever with sending numerical messages like typing: 07734, when turned upside down it looks like HELLO. We also sent encrypted messages that only meant something to you and the person who sent it. The pagers got much bigger and the technology also increased. Then we were able to send emails and verbal messages to the beeper.

The Foundational Era of rap music was the start of hip-hop rap culture as we know it today. It also was a gateway introduction to much of the pop culture we follow today. Around the time that the Foundational Era rappers were blowing up, the first mention of a cellphone was used in lyrics or photoshoots and album covers. The brick cellphone, as it was affectionately called because it was the size and shape of a brick, was the first portable cell phone available to the public. Back then, only a very few people could afford a brick cell phone because they were so expensive. We saw people in the movies and on Wall Street using these phones; but very few people in the hood had one. It was rumored that a well-known drug kingpin in my hood had one of these phones; but I did not know him well enough to know if this was true. As we got deeper into the Golden Era of Rap the cellphones became smaller and more affordable. The flip phone is invented and introduced to the public. The phone was much smaller than the brick phone and was more affordable. This is when your local drug dealers started having cellphones in the community; but still the initial rollout of these phones were too expensive for the working-class citizen to purchase. Once these phones hit the black market, everybody and they momma had them a cell phone with the illegal chip in it. Flashing one of those phones, at a bus stop in the early 90s, was the quickest way to impress a young lady. The phone was such an alluring item that you really did not have to have any service on it. Just holding the phone alone was enough to attract the intended target.

As we cruised through the Golden Era into the Millennial era, the cellphones just got more sophisticated. They started with allowing the users to text one another, then they created the smart phone. Next, the phones were equipped with cameras and the ability to check emails from your phone. Today, the cellphones are miniature computers we carry around on our person. The phones have data that is equivalent to some tablets and laptops. I personally stopped at texting, and still use it as my main way of communicating through my smartphone. The cellphones became better as time progressed, unfortunately, the same cannot be said for rap music. The quality of the rap music today seemed to lessen from that of the previous rap eras. There are some Zoomer Era rappers who does stand out from the pack; they seem to have what it takes to make quality rap music. Most of the rappers today seemed to follow a mantra of only being in the game for the money. While this may be true for most artist, the true artist realize that they would be rapping even if just for hobby. The love of the music must be first in the mind of a true artist. The money will follow if an artist is true to his art. Today successful rap artists are created by the business-of-rap machine. They market the artist to a certain demographic, develop a fanbase; and sell you the fantasy of the artist's story. This is the reason why we see new rappers perpetrating a gangster image to gain a following.

TRACK# 36: SMOOVED OUT

As the 20th century came to an end, rap music had reached its commercial height! Rappers were now doing records with R&B acts to get a carryover sound for the radio. The game began to soften its message and it allowed rappers from all backgrounds to enter. The white rappers were now able to angle themselves back into the rap game. Just like in boxing, the white community has always looked for a Great White Hope (GWH). The phrase, Great White Hope, was taken from the sport of boxing. It was coined as such because the white community desperately wanted someone to beat the black heavyweight champion of the time. So, the first white artist with a semblance of complex rhyme patterns would be thrust as the best thing since sliced bread. This happened in the early 2000s; and it also began the start of the separation of the rap fan. Like professional boxing in the US, the fans love a black champion fighter when he's facing another black fighter; but they easily go against the black boxing champion when he's fighting against someone from another race. In the early stages of rap, kids of all ethnicities bought rap records because of the music, and not because they felt a certain kinship to the artist. They were rappers from all ethnicities in the beginning stages of rap. white, black, and Latin ethnic artists were involved in all four elements of hip-hop. As time would pass, and rap was becoming more mainstream; consumers wanted to hold up hip-hop artists who looked like them. Both, white and Latin consumers wanted someone from their cultural background to be crowned the king of rap. With having a white rapper at the top of the game, came a plethora of casual white rap fans. These white rap fans, looking to be the best at something black related, quickly anointed the white rapper as the G.O.A.T. or simply written GOAT ... Greatest Of All Time! Of course, this would cause dissension amongst the regular rap fans. Now white rap fans felt compelled to diss black artists they used to show support to; and black rap supporters felt they had no choice but to reciprocate.

Caveat Interlude:
Side note: I particularly thought that the Great White Hope was and is a very good rapper; but because of the extreme hype surrounding him, I did not thoroughly listen to all his music. Contrary to what one might think; during this time, they were several black rap fans who supported the GWH! Some even went overboard to show that they did not feel the same as some of their black contemporaries who felt that he was not the GOAT. These black rap fans praised the GWH more than his white fans did. They argued in his defense on message boards. Some even stated that non-supporters of the GWH were being racist if they did not agree with their opinion. Black people have always felt the need to protect white people who either lived or visited our communities.

In the past, white rappers would enter the music industry through rap and once their career began to fizzle, they would ease over into more culturally associated white genres of music like country or rock. This was usually what happened to those white emcees who tried to sound too Black. Things changed once the GWH surfaced, thus allowing him to stay around longer in the rap game. He was backed by one of the greatest producers in rap, who just happened to be a black man. The GWH would be cemented in the Hip-Hop community as one of the GOATS by all ethnicities involved in the rap music industry. This ideal of having someone who look like you to represent you in the music is common across all genres of music. This is true in life as well; people gravitate to what they know or what makes them comfortable. So, it was only a matter of time before rappers began to appear from different cultures.

Fast forward to today, many of the top selling rappers are white artists. Some of them do not even consider themselves to be rappers; but they continue to make money off the genre. As the founding fathers of rap began to age; their offspring allowed the industry to be infiltrated by anyone who wanted to enter. The older black fans began to believe that hip-hop, or rap for that matter, was dead. Many of the top black artists lead campaigns to express their disdain with the current state of hip-hop. What had started out as a way for young black ghetto kids to escape poverty, was now being mainstreamed and taken over by white artists. Sounds familiar rock and roll? It was not that hip-hop was dead, it was more that the white consumers, who usually purchased all hip-hop artists in large numbers, were no longer supporting black artists like they had in the past. This change was not due to white fans no longer liking the music; it was because they preferred that the artists making the music looked like them. Today, they now have their pick of the litter of white rappers who can somewhat rap!

TRACK #37: THE RAP RACE
(The Millennial Era, cont.)

The Millennial Era would see the solo rapper catapulted into the stratosphere of hip-hop! This spawned the era of decadence and excess! The diamonds became blingier and the automobiles purchased were gaudier. Jewelers became stars and European car dealerships thrived as these artists began to make more money than they ever imagined! The rap star was becoming the pop star in the U.S. The budgets were getting bigger! The entourage grew thicker! The groupies became more accessible! The emcee was able to parlay his celebrity into many different entertainment avenues. During this era, you saw rappers turn into movie stars. They became household names! The professional athlete began to lend their voices to the rap game. The music videos grew bigger and "Deffer"! Rap music had become the most popular genre of music for the youths around the world. Every demographic, young and old, had begun to accept rap as a legitimate art form.

Rap music was now in the suburbs of white America! The offspring of the conservative white male had become infatuated with the rebellious nature of the lyrics that most rappers used in their music. This phenomenon helped spike the sales of rap music. The Golden Era saw some of the first multi-platinum rap artist make a serious impact in the business of rap. The Millennial Era continued where the Golden Era left off; and introduced multiple rap artists to the platinum sales club. This era also spawned white rap artists who would go on to surpass the black rap artist in record sales. Sidebar: *I personally never judge the talent of an artist by their record sales. Therefore, it makes logical sense that a popular white rapper would sell more records than any black rap artist because the white consumers were responsible for the large record sales! I digress!*

The rapper was now the face of the hip-hop industry. Everyone wanted to become a rapper! It was a job that could make you instantly rich and famous. You could become a true overnight celebrity; and many people looked at the profession as an easy way out of poverty. The rags-to-riches story that many rap artists articulated was usually embellished a tad bit to help drive record sales. Many of the artists who would eventually reach the ears of the mainstream rap fans had probably been grinding on the underground scene for years before they blew up. I like to call this the 'Bamboo Tree Effect'; meaning: Like a Chinese bamboo tree grows for years underground before it breaks through the surface, the underground rapper would follow the same trajectory. And, like a bamboo tree, once it breaks ground, it reaches a maximum height in a very short time. This newfound stardom could make or break a new artist coming from dismal backgrounds (there is a reason it is called the sophomore jinx). Or, they had prior connections which allowed them to jump over the barriers-to-entry that most lay artists did not have. During this era, everyone wanted to be a rapper! Athletes, Actors, and other professionals of the arts wanted to make a rap record. The rappers had become the rock stars of the time. Rappers were as cool as the jazz artists of the Sixties! Only now, you did not have to have much talent to make a hit record! Rap music had become ubiquitous throughout the world; and rap stars took advantage of their fame.

CHAPTER #38: THE MUMBLE JUNGLE
(The Zoomer Era)

As the popularity of rap music would continue to grow, the skills required to make a hit record would diminish. The necessary knowledge that was required to make a hit record before had now become obsolete. Technology had become the great equalizer in the rap music industry. Rappers were able to make or buy beats from someone online to make their records. The popularity of the song began to be more about the beat than the potency of the lyrics. To make a hit record required that you had a certain type of beat and sound. Certain music producers became the "go-to" person if you wanted your artist to have that sound. Thus, the producer would move to the forefront of making hit rap records. The Zoomers would pick up where the Millennials left off making less boom bap sounding rap music. The soundscapes were lusher, and the lyrical subject matter was much softer. The fusion of rap and R&B was the new sound being played on mainstream terrestrial radio. The radio personalities had to stick to the "programming" of the radio station, thus, less street underground music was played on the airwaves. This allowed subpar rappers to enter the rap game without any turbulence from the rap gods.

One of the main reasons rap lyrics became less prolific was because of how formulaic it became to make a hit record. This was due to how much weight was now placed on having a certain type of beat to drive the record. This copycat template was not new to the rap industry. In fact, once rap became popular music; the songs heard on the radio began sounding similar. This is when many R&B artists began infusing hip-hop style beats into their music. Even the white pop artists realized how powerful rap music had become, and they started using hip-hop beats in their music as well. Contrarily, we still had some variety to choose from on the pop radio during the Golden and Millennial Eras of rap. During the Zoomer Era of rap music, the beat was now king. Artist could literally say anything in their songs and still make a hit record because of how dope the beat was. In fact, a new genre of rap was created during this era of hip-hop. It was coined "Mumble Rap" because the artists literally sounded like they were mumbling when they were rapping over the beats.

The rap music producer proved that, through it all, the music is still king. They started to ascend during the Millennial Era of rap, and they are still climbing in the Zoomer Era today. If you want a radio hit; you hire a certain producer or get a similar sounding track from a lesser known one. It is truly all about the beat! Even the rappers from the older eras of music understand that lyrical content is not as important. Contrarily, the most successful rappers of this era all have the gift of lyricism. They have found a way to make music for the casual fan and the hardcore backpacker. These artists walk a thin line like a trapeze artist holding a balancing stick with trap beats on one side and backpack lyrics on the other. They are the artist that everyone in the household know of; both old and young.

The Zoomers have developed a few new artists who stand out from the pack. A couple of these "Babies" have developed a core audience and they have mastered the art of creating hit records. When you listen closely to their music, you can hear the influence from previous eras of rap. You can tell that they were brought up by parents who listened to rap from the Golden Era and beyond. Trouble comes with fame and stardom, and the Zoomer Era rappers are no different than past era rappers. Yet, I also see the activism and undisturbed bravery that some of them also exhibit. I see the potential for them to become the vanguards of future generations of the rap game. I hope that they can rekindle the magic of the past eras of rap music. I truly want the best for them!

TRACK #39: ALPHABET, ALGEBRA, HIEROGLYPHICS

The Foundational Era of rap music saw some of the most diverse rap artists the rap industry has ever seen. It started out with rappers who only got a chance to rhyme between the records the DJ played. Then it morphed into the emcee being the front man and rapping over sampled beats from older jazz and blues records. Then it would venture into rappers perfecting their rhyme styles and subject matter. Currently it is in a state of shock and awe with rappers making music they think will be polarizing. In the beginning of rap music, the rhymes that most used were very simplistic. There were artists who were clearly novelty acts pushed to help sell the culture. Some of the first rap stars were artists who were placed in their position because of who they knew and how they were able to deliver the message. The rap songs of these artist had lyrics that were very simplistic and elementary in nature. Contrarily, there were rappers in this era that pushed the lyrical envelope because of their natural rhyming ability; but these rappers were few and far between.

Towards the tail end of the Foundational Era of rap, artists began to make more complicated rhyme schemes. The subject matter of the songs allowed these artists to become the leaders of the rap industry during that time. A few of the Foundational Era rappers would make music that would shift the rhyme paradigm forever. These artists made music that focused on the rapper's ability to write intricate and clever rhymes. It made it so that anyone looking to enter the rap game had to really focus on what they were writing. These artists made rhyming an artform that helped further push the cause of rap being a legitimate genre of music. This poetry of metaphors and similes would get even better during the Golden Era of rap music. Those rappers of the Golden Era would build on the foundation that was in place when they entered the rap game. The rhymes were much more complicated, and the storylines were much more detailed. The enhancement of the raps, coupled with getting signed to a label, made it much more difficult for any Joe Blow to enter the game. The Golden Era is when the songs became more formulaic; and the structure was set in place as a template for future rap artists to use.

The Millennial Era rappers would pick-up what the Golden Era rappers had started. They would continue to build the genre up by making chart topping records that moved the entire world. The music had become an international success; and rap artists were the biggest pop stars of the time. The Southern region of the USA rappers were now running the rap game. The lyrical content became less metaphorical and the subject matter was more in your face. The rap CEOs of the South allowed for true street hustlers to enter the rap game. Trap Rap, although a few great rappers emerged from it, allowed the street hustler to talk fly shit on records about his life in the dope game. The dumbing down of the music would begin to spread to all regions on the map. Then Mumble Rap would emerge and rappers from the East and West started mimicking the Southern Mumble Rappers styled. As I mentioned before, the rap business is a copycat industry. When Mumble Rap became the hot new trend, I can honestly say that I could no longer relate or understand what the rapper was saying in his song. If it were not for the hook, I probably would not know what the song was about. It was as if these rap artists were speaking a different language. Like most records on the radio that are repeated over-and-over again, I begun to understand what the artists were saying. Some of the music was really good, and the lyrics were on par with some of the best I had ever heard. I just had to slow things down a bit, and really focused on the pronunciation and the enunciation of the rhymes they were spittin. I say all of this to say, give the youth a chance. Understand that our elders did not understand or like rap music when they first heard it. If the music is still important to you; sit still and translate it. If not, subscribe to satellite radio, they still play the old school joints.

TRACK #40: THE OUTRO

There is a common thread that is pervasive through each era of rap music. Well, there are two common threads that I noticed in every rap era. The first thread is that the freshmen rappers of every era, with longevity potential in the game, studied those that came before them. These artists combined what they learned from the past with what was currently happening during their era of the rap game. This duality allowed them to play in both worlds and cater to both the old and new generations. These artists are the ones who would eventually rise to the top of their rap class; and were able to maintain staying power in the game. It is quite likely that these rappers are still around today.

The other types are the new artist that only rep their era of rap music. These artists came into the game without studying the artists who came before them. Most of these artists inundated themselves with the current trends and fads that represented their culture. They are the ones who, if you took a snapshot of them at their apex, looked like the poster child of their era. They were the vanguards of their era; and typically, were the ones who were quick to call the pass era rapper "old school". You could find quotes from most of them either dissing or blatantly showing disrespect for those who came before them. These rappers typically get a hot single and try to live off that alone. Rarely do these types last longer than their sophomore albums; and that is if they even got a second chance. One would think that these artists would have learned the game by now. Or, that one of their record company execs would have given them the game. Most of the freshmen artists are young and naïve to how the rap industry work. Most of them are so eager to escape poverty that they end up signing poor contracts with unscrupulous people in the music industry. They, like many young athletes, are given too much too soon at an early age. The accolades are mostly given off their potential to become successful in their profession. Many of them never reach their full potential because of the false praise and rewards handed to them. These are the ones running around with 'Yes Men' who are too afraid to give them the real!

In the current state of rap today, Zoomer Era, it is too difficult to determine what is considered real anymore. Artists can perpetrate their gangsterism personas well enough to gain the support of millions of followers. Even with smoking gun proof of their falsities, they can overcome any accusations thrown their way. Once fandom is developed for an artist, it is almost impossible to convince them of anything they do not want to believe. Their celebrity brings enough people around to support the façade, and eventually the artist began to believe his own lies. Too many times these artists end with more chaos in their lives than what they came into the rap game with. These artists start out with a clean slate but leave with a criminal history. While studying all eras of rap music, I realized that the fake wannabe gangster has been around throughout rap's hip-hop history. Some of these artists were posers, some had not fully developed into who they would become, and for some, they finally got caught in the act. In either case, there have been several artists who waited to become famous before committing their first crime!

The rap elements I chose to base this book around have existed from the origins of hip-hop rap music. Drug Culture, Criminality, Attention, and Popularity are cornerstones in rap music and culture. Every form of rap pulls something from one of the rap elements. From backpacker to party rap, from conscious to gangster, they center their foundation around one of the elements. History is bound to repeat itself, thus causing a sense of déjà vu. Era after era we see the same types of rappers entering the rap game with subtle differences that represent the current climate of the world. Technology has changed a few things in the culture, but in the end, it is still about the rapper's skill and ability to create music that correlates with the present time. As hip-hop rap music matures and heads towards its golden anniversary, ageism has decreased in each era. Rappers from the origins of the game are still performing and making music today. There is a lane for these artists that did not seem to be in the earlier years of rap music. If you are a real fan and supporter of an "Old School" artist, then you know that many are still releasing new music today.

The future is bright for hip-hop rap music! It is now one of the most popular genres of music in the world. The diversity in rap music has helped it spread into homes around the globe. It is truly the vanguard of popular music today! Since its inception, there have been new categories created in rap music. These new categories include both, sacred and secular forms of the music. There are now gospel, country, and Latin rap music being performed by artists in these genres. The music is being scored for movies and you hear some form of hip-hop in almost every new commercial. What was once something that many music pundits said would not last, is now the leader of the new school of music. I am proud to say that I passed down to my kids what a true emcee should sound like. They understand that you do not have to like every type of rap or every song that their favorite artist drop. Variety is needed in rap music because we all have cultural differences that make the music more relatable to us; and it gives us the opportunity to learn from each other. Rap music has taught me that change is inevitable; and that you must know where you come from to get to where you want to go. I never thought that rap music would be this big! We went from not having an award category, to having an entire award show dedicated to the artform. I honor and respect rappers of all races and ethnicities; and I encourage anyone to participate. Just make sure you pay your respects to those that came before and make music that will continue pushing the culture forward. Currently we have rappers who represent all races and ethnic groups in America. My International rappers, we hear you, and I look forward to hearing and learning more.

I leave you with this: We must learn from our past mistakes to ensure a brighter future for everyone. We can all love something equally, share the same space, and be different simultaneously! We must not allow our personal beliefs and dogmatic systems to stifle the growth of the whole. We cannot stop time, and positive change is imminent! Love conquers All! Rap music is Love! Hip-Hop Lives Forever!

BONUS TRACKS: SONGS THAT DID NOT MAKE THE ALBUM

Track 1: Cancel Culture

Cancel culture is when a celebrity does something that their fanbase does not agree with, and then the fanbase deem them no longer important to the culture. The disagreement can be something political or just against what is considered the norm; and their fans will stop supporting them all together. This cancel culture started when social media became available to the public. Before social media, the average rap fan only knew what the rapper portrayed in their music. The daily livelihoods of the rapper celebrity were not available to their fanbases. We assumed that all superstar rappers lived exactly like the images we saw in their videos. Once social media became a platform that all artist had to partake in, we were able to see that many of these celebrities lived normal mundane lives. This also opened the communication channels between the artist and the fans. Many celebrities began to truly express how they felt about social and political issues. Unfortunately for some celebrities their opinions were not popular with their core fan base, and it cost them casual fans and some of their core fans.

In the black community we are quick to cancel a celebrity if their opinion is not congruent with the popular opinion of the majority. This is especially true when discussing African American social-political issues. If a black celebrity has a different opinion about a subject, one we assume all black people should support, then we automatically label them a coon and possibly cancel them as one of ours. Although this may seem harsh on the surface, I understand why we take our celebrities opinions so seriously. For one, as a black race in America, we have very little culture to call our own. Secondly, we treat all black people like extended family members, so quite naturally we feel some type of way when our family goes against us. Thirdly, as a race we try not to air our dirty laundry, so we feel betrayed when a black celebrity talks out against the majority opinion. And finally, we hold the opinions of celebrities in high esteem, so a differing opinion from a black celebrity may force us to change our original thoughts about the subject. Cancel Culture became a thing during the Millennial Era of rap, and it continues until today!

Track 2: A Nothing Celebrity

The Millennial Era of rap will go down in history as one that spearheaded a lot of the culture that we currently see in the world today. It was also an era that created new avenues for individuals to become celebrities without much effort and having little to no talent. This was a time when heiresses of wealthy families became socialites and leveraged their popularity into becoming a celebrity. The trajectory of their stardom usually started with a leaked sex tape that they pretended to be unaware of. Then, they begin appearing at certain celebrity events. Then, out-of-the-blue, BAM, they get their own television show. This leads them into endorsements, businesses, and other lucrative joint ventures that helped further solidify their celebrity. When the dust settled, and you take a serious look at their career, you then realize that they became a celebrity without having any skill or talent. Besides having the ability to anonymously leak a sex tape, what else do they do? Some of them may come in under the guise of being a quasi-model. Consequently, they do not become famous from modeling.

Today we have internet models who make their way into celebrity by doing unscrupulous sexual acts on social media sites. These modern-day courtesans used their assets to attract, and sometimes entrap, already famous men. Most of them are women who were at one time strippers; basically, they left the pole for the laptop. Those who are more risqué eventually begin selling pornography on their own personal websites. The men garner attention similarly by attention whoring in different ways. Some make lewd unfunny videos, while others just behave belligerently in front of a camera. Most of these men label themselves as internet comedians or entertainers. The ideal behind their shenanigans is to gain as many followers as they can on their social media platforms. Then, hopefully, they can parlay their popularity into earning advertising dollars. This hustle has created new online professions that could not exist before. On one hand you can say that these people are creative geniuses; on the other you can say that they do nothing special to warrant their celebrity. They are now new professions like: Influencers, Bloggers, and Fashionistas. Most celebrities become famous by mastering their art and being the best in their field. These new online celebrities are truly famous because of the number of followers they have, and nothing else. Hey, who am I to knock their hustle!

I would be remised, because of cancel culture, if I did not say that "Not All" of these online personalities are talentless. Some of the internet comedians are truly funny and they deserve to get all the attention they get. Some of the internet models are truly using social media to bolster their careers into modeling and other avenues of entertainment, not all of them are ex-strippers. I follow the good ones I come across on social media. I believe that these certain individuals would have made it regardless of their internet presence. I have learned from them how to use social media as a marketing tool. I applaud those who do it the correct way. Then again, is there an incorrect way?

Track 3: Pick Your Poison

The music profession has always been associated with alcohol and some form of drug consumption! From the very beginning of the secular forms of music being sold as a product, there have been artists who indulged in one of the vices. We all know of the past Rock n Roll, Jazz, and in recent years, the rap artists who died because of their overindulgence in drugs. We know of the stories from the past of how musicians abused alcohol and made life hell for themselves and those around them. Well before hip-hop was thought about, musicians of other genres used and abused drugs and alcohol. In the 60s, the bebop jazz artists shot-up heroine to help them formulate their cool. Simultaneously, the rockers did the same while snorting cocaine for recreation. Several of our musical icons throughout history died from overdosing some form of drug. The list goes on-and-on, regardless of the musical genre, some of the biggest stars partied hard and died young from overindulging in drugs.

In recent years, starting with the Golden Era of rap, rap stars have lost their struggles to drug addiction. The deadly drug of choice around this time was some form of cocaine or opioids. I can remember growing up in the 90s, and the rappers and the movies promoted malt liquor beer. We ran to our local corner store to buy 40 oz bottles of this extremely high alcohol content beer. We drunk it throughout high school and as young men in the hood. For a small moment in time, drinking 40ozs surpassed smoking cigarettes as a rite of passage for young teens in the hood. Yet, the recreational drug of choice for most adolescent age kids was still marijuana. West coast rappers helped encourage the use of the plant; and teens throughout the world began to indulge in its allure.

The Golden Era phased into the Millennial Era and rappers started using codeine as a deadly drug choice. The combination of drinking liquid codeine and smoking marijuana together deemed too much for the heart to handle. As the Millennial Era merged into the Zoomer Era, the use of drugs in the form of pills became popular. We started to hear of rappers OD'ing from popping too many pills. We recently lost a couple of young talented rap artist because of cocktailing too many types of drugs. What is it that make our most talented artist gravitate to using deadly drugs? Why do many of our rap stars glorify the use of drugs in their music? One might can argue that many of the artists are young and they are rapping about what they know. Others might say that there is an agenda behind promoting artist who rap about using drugs. Still some might say that it is just the young folk feeling like they are invincible.

Woven throughout the history of using deadly drugs is the use of marijuana. Although, there is no history of anyone dying from using marijuana; many may argue that it is a gateway into using more deadly forms of drugs. In recent years, independent marijuana growers have been creating strains of the drug with much higher THC levels. One might can argue that individuals may not be in their right minds when smoking such high levels THC. See Warning: Do not operate large machinery while under the influence. Being under the influence of marijuana can cause one to have delayed reactions and poor judgment. Thus, severe accidents, and even death, can be caused when driving or doing other things that require our maximum attention, while under the influence of this new "Loud" weed.

Track 4: Colorism

I was born in a city where being a certain color of skin played a major role in your success. I grew up in a city of black people who self-identified as being Creole or Cajun. Most of these individuals had French surnames and practiced Catholicism. Their family trees extended back to the Louisiana Purchase where free blacks were treated better because of their mixed-race heritage. Many of these free black's origins were Africans who fled Haiti after the Revolution, Africans who were Native to the land, or those brought in through Slave trading. These Africans had babies with French and Spanish settlers, who were probably slave owners, and created a separate ethnic group of mixed-raced kids. These kids grew up as free blacks and they developed the same cultural practices as their parents. They were treated different than their unmixed African peers and were given special privileges. Consequently, the free blacks treated the non-free blacks just like their parents did their slaves. Fast forward to my upbringing in the city of New Orleans. I can remember the lighter complexion kids, regardless of their heritage, making fun and ridiculing the darker complexion kids because of their skin color. This type of teasing caused many dark complexion kids to have an inferiority complex to those with a lighter skin complexion. Contrarily, the lighter complexion kids grew up with a superiority complex, thus causing them to act the same as adults they observed growing up.

I believe I was in the 5th grade when I first started paying attention to rap music. I immediately fell in love with the idea of putting poetry over melodic beats. I was way too shy to dance, or to freestyle in front of a crowd; so, I concentrated on writing the flyest rhymes I could think of. Back then there were not many rap music videos on regular network television. We were relegated to watching weekly countdown video shows that only showcased rock n roll videos. Consequently, I am a huge fan of 80s rock music. By the time I got to high school in the early 90s, the rap music industry was in full swing and there were plenty music videos broadcasting on some form of television programming. Being a young virile teenager, the first thing I noticed about the videos were the women. The women in the videos were all very pretty and voluptuous. The earlier videos showcased women of all races and colors; but as time would progress, I noticed a pattern in the videos. Most of the video vixens casted in the rap videos had very fair complexions or had an exotic look about them. Some of these women were not black women, and those with different cultural backgrounds did not identify as being black. Yet, the rappers rapped as if they were talking about girls in their community. During the Millennial Era of rap, many of the top artists boasted about desiring a fair complexion or exotic looking woman. These same artists have dark skin mothers, aunts, and sisters, some even have dark complexion daughters. Yet, they only brag, lust for, and uphold the fairer complexion women! There is a lot that can be said for the reasoning behind these artists way of thinking when it comes to their choice of women; but I will save that topic for a different book.

Track 5: Black Girl Dolls

The 80s can be remembered as a decade of flashy things and decadence! Everything in the 80s was new and groundbreaking. The television sitcoms of the 80s were written well, and many are considered classics today. The movies seemed bigger and bolder; and the movie stars shined brighter. The Hollywood lifestyle was portrayed for all to see; and the American populace quickly picked-up and mimicked what they saw. The guys were running around wearing designer sunglasses and driving droptop sport sedans; and the women filled their bikinis with fake double D breast implants while showcasing their perfectly shaped nose jobs. Does any of this sound familiar to how you grew up in the 80s? Well, if you are a black person who grew up during the 80s, none of this sounds familiar. For most black people who were old enough to pay taxes in the 80s, none of the above luxuries seemed possible. In fact, most blacks were still getting over the damages the Jim Crow laws caused, and many still suffered mentally, causing post trauma. Add to the fact that most black men were absent (dead, imprisoned, deadbeat); thus, causing a scarcity of family life in the black community. To put it simply, we could not afford such luxuries! But I digress!

I grew up in a very religious household and studied under Christianity. White Jesus played the role of a stepfather to many of the single and widowed black mothers in the hood. Because of our religious beliefs, certain things were considered taboo in our community. One of these taboo things were getting cosmetic surgery, or as we called it, plastic surgery done to any part of your body. It was almost sacrileges to have doctors to cut on your body for the sole purpose of vanity. At some point in time, the ideals of the past began to change. The female rappers of the

Foundational and Golden Era of rap music never rapped about getting any body enhancements. If they did get anything done; the public was never privy to that information. As the Golden Era of rap waned and the female rappers of the Millennial Era began to take centerstage, the subject matter started to change significantly. Now female rappers started to rap about getting their breasts done, ass lifts, tummy tucks, and getting shots to smooth out their wrinkles. Like most trends, the "black" market eventually develops a generic form of the most trending thing to capitalize on. This is when we began hearing about women getting butt injections from unlicensed people in their homes. This market skyrocketed, and before you knew it, every black girl on social media had some type of cosmetic enhancement done on their bodies.

Today it is a normal procedure for black women to have some type of cosmetic surgery done on their person. What was once taboo is now the norm in black society today. This paradigm shift in thinking could be because of a couple of cultural shifts in the black community. One is that, in recent years black women have become the most educated of any ethnic group. Thus, allowing them to have access to more discretionary income and medical insurance coverage to have cosmetic surgery. This was not available in the past because of their lack of funds. Another reason could be that several black females in entertainment have openly admitted to having something done to enhance their looks. For those who refuse to admit to having work done, the physical changes in their faces are a dead giveaway. Being that we are such a copycat society, it easily understandable to see why young black girls want to change their appearance. So, black women are now doing whatever it takes to look like a plastic doll. Contrarily, white women are getting butt implants and lip injections to look like black women. Crazy, mixed-up world, right!

Track 6: Social Media

I heard a Millennial Era rapper say that the rappers from the past eras of rap would not survive in the current rap climate because of social media. His reasoning behind the bar in his rhyme was, he believed that social media has made it too easy to reveal the skeletons in their closets. His assumption was that the rappers of the past could not deal with the pressures of having their lives play-out in front of their fans. He was pontificating that, somehow the current rap superstar artists are better in some way because they can survive in this information era. It was almost as if he was juxtaposing the job of a rapper with that of a politician. So, I began to give this belief some thought. For those living under a rock: Social Media are the apps and internet sites that allow users to post up pictures, images, videos, and messages about almost anything. It gives their fans a way to communicate with the artist. These users are usually posting up material about themselves. They show their own personal lives on these platforms, and none of them are coerced or forced into putting up the material. I do understand that there are paparazzi snapping pictures and putting them up on sites and selling them to magazines. I also realize that there are gossip sites and magazines writing negative articles and spreading negative information about these artists. But, most of the damage caused is self-inflicted by the artist themselves.

My conjecture about the artists of the past is that the smart ones would be able to adapt to any climate. I am certain that if social media were around back then we would know the same information about those artists that we know now. The difference would be that the information would be available quicker; but we would know all the same. Social media, and paparazzi for that matter, is designed to give the fans an up-close view of the life of a celebrity. I believe that most celebrities suffer from narcissism and having the ability to read what their fans think about them could deem difficult. When you are in the eye of the public, you must have thick skin. In fact, the rappers from the Foundational and Golden Eras participate in social media today. They only post enough to keep their fans interested. Anything they do not want us to know about, they do not post it. I follow most of these artists, and I only know of the information they make public. So theoretically, the artist from the past era of rap are doing just fine in this social media era. I wonder if the current rap artist would have survived the prior era of rap music. What do you think?

Track #7: They Say It, Why Can't I?

In a previous chapter in the book, I mentioned how the rappers in the current era of music have allowed their friends to use the dreaded N-word. Well, as bad as that is, other ethnic groups believing that they should be allowed to say it because we do, is even worse. The idea that you should be allowed to use a racial slur because people of that race uses the word is ludicrous. An example would be that a non-Italian person would argue with someone who is Italian for the right to call them a racial slur that is offensive to Italian people. The Italian person would automatically be offended; but the non-Italian person would not ever consider doing such.

    I am certain that the hip-hop culture is complicit in making ethnic groups outside of the black race think that it is okay to use the word. I know that the rap music is infused with the word on almost every song. I also know that most rappers who are African American use the word as a term of endearment and not as a form of slander. I also realize that many groups who are ethnically black, but not culturally black, may get a pass to use the word. I am leery of those historically ethnically black groups of people who pretend to really be down for the black race, but ridicule and hate us in private. I personally do not believe in giving a pass to anyone outside of the African American race and culture. I tend not to use the word when I am not around the groups of people that I am okay with using it in front of me. I try not to seem triggered around those historically ethnic groups who use the word in my presence. I just quickly remove myself from the situation or address my disdain for the use of the word. Anybody who is not from the black race should feel ashamed using the word at all. I know that everything is not for everybody, and you should too!

Track#8: Latin Connection

The Latin influence in the beginning of hip-hop culture is sometimes overlooked. The Puerto Ricans and Caribbean Latinos were and is a major part of the inner cities of New York. As hip-hop developed and turned into an artform, many Latinos played a major part in cultivating the culture. Many Latinos, who were around from the origins of rap, longed for someone who represented them in the music as well. Throughout the history of rap and up to the present there have been several dope Latin rappers in the game. The West coast had the Mexican rappers who would make their imprint in the rap game. Most of the early rappers of any Latino heritage (Afro-Latinos) usually represented their African roots when they participated in the rap industry. Many Latinos who participated in the origins of hip-hop were usually into break dancing or B-boying. They found their niche to be a part of the hip-hop movement that their neighborhood African American peers all participated in.

Breakdancing was a major part of the hip-hop culture in the early eighties. Ghettos across the U.S. had teenagers cutting open large cardboard boxes to break dance on. The dancers who became masters of their craft were call B-Boys and B-Girls. They formulated crews who would battle each other for supremacy in the breakdancing arena. On the West coast, pop locking would become their version of break dancing amongst the young street kids growing up in California. I remember running to the corner store and searching behind their trash dumpster for used cardboard boxes. We would gather all the cardboard we could find and duct tape them together to make a smooth surface to protect our bones from the concrete when we danced. My friends and I took them to the back of the scattered-sites, and we all attempted to do our best imitation of the breakers we saw in the movies. Breakdancing was only a fad in our community. We would eventually develop our own dances and style of music that was deeply rooted in our culture. It was mostly call-and-response type of dances where the MC would shout out various local dances and the crowd would comply. Today break dancers have become less a part of the forefront of the hip-hop community in the U.S. Many of the original break dancers have found more support in the artform across seas.

Track# 9: It Takes Money to Make Money (Aka Play for Pay) (Payola)

You ever wondered why certain rappers and rap groups were able to blow up and get radio airplay and others could not? Have you ever heard a song on the radio that was so horrible that you could not believe what you were hearing? Well, you are not alone because throughout the history of rap music I too sometimes wondered why such distasteful songs were allowed on the radio. Yet, we must admit, after hearing the song for the umpteenth time, you began thinking is was jamming. I was once an aspiring rapper on the local scene in New Orleans. I watched other local rap stars sign to local labels and blow up. Some of them would become known around the world and go on to become local rap legends. I tried to create my own label and would bring songs to get played on the radio station only to get the run around. I knew that the music I was creating was much better than most of the songs being played on the radio; but somehow these artists were still able to get radio airplay. I still could not just believe that their music was that much better than mine. We would give out our music in the hoods and get good responses from the listeners. I even went to some of the local rap stars and asked them about the process of getting their music on the radio. I usually got looks of confusion, which usually meant that they didn't know or that look that said: If you don't already know, I ain't telling ya! Something just wasn't adding up.

I noticed that every artist on the radio was signed to a label, whether local or national. So, I started researching how these labels operated, and what type of business they were doing to be so successful. There was one common denominator that is common in startup business in all sectors, and this was money. Not only did the labels have money to start; but they had to have lots of it. Then I started breaking down the expenses a record label could incur; and these were the usual things like: studio cost, travel, pressing the CD's, etc. But there was one expense that was usually lumped into miscellaneous or just included in the liabilities as radio expenses. This radio expense would be sold as the artists doing radio interviews while going on a press run; but missing from those expenditures were the payola that was paid to the radio station itself and the disc jockeys playing those records. It is the reason that some artists have regional success while others were able to go national. This was also called breaking a record in a certain market. This is the reason that you hear the same 8 to 10 records being played on the radio stations daily. This is the reason why artists were so desperately looking to sign to a label back in the day. These labels were able to front the money to get these artist's careers off the ground. I could go on and on about how payola helped changed the rap game to the state that it is currently in today; but I think those with deep understanding will get it. Money will always talk in a land where capitalism is still king. It makes one question if we have really heard the best of the best emcee.

GLOSSARY

All words are defined in the author's own words and based on how he uses them in the book)
Words are alphabetized

Bamboo Tree Effect: *Is based on the concept of the Chinese bamboo plant that grows underground for 5-years before breaking the surface. Once it breaks the surface, it grows to maximum heights in a very little time.*

Bar: *In rap music, equals one measure of written lyrics out of the typical 16.*

B Boy: *Is short for Breaking Boy, or male break dancer.*

B Girl: *Is short for Breaking Girl, or female break dancer.*

Blunts: *A cigar that is cut open, tobacco thrown away, and filled with marijuana.*

Boom Bap: *Golden Era east coast rap music with heavy bass beats.*

Bootleg Man: *A person who sells faux merchandise for a profit.*

Chatty Patties: *A person who gossips and tells everyone's business.*

Chocolate Thai: *A type of marijuana strain.*

Chucks: *Converse Chuck Taylor sneakers.*

Clout Chasing: *When someone does something to get attention from someone more famous or popular than them in hopes that they will respond so they could ride their stardom and fame.*

Compact Cassette: *A medium that stored music to play in a device. Search Compact Cassette for image.*

Compact Disc: *A medium that stored music to play in a device. Search Compact Disc for image.*

Coon: *Typically, A black person who does not support his race when discussing racial issues.*

Dabbing: *A different way to smoke concentrated forms of marijuana in a vaporizer or bong.*

Deffer: *Slang terminology meaning that something is better.*
Dime Rock: *Small piece of crack cocaine named because of the $10 price tag.*

Drop: *Release date or time when music is scheduled to be available to the public.*

Dub Sack: *A $20 bag of marijuana.*

Eight Ball or 8-Ball: *An eighth of an ounce of cocaine.*

Eight Track or 8-Track: *A medium that stored music to play in a device. Search 8-Track for image.*

Emcee: *An emcee is a play on the words MC (Masters of Ceremony), the MC is the rapper in the hip-hop outfit.*

Flava or Flavor: *As used in the book, to put something extra into something that is already good.*

Fly or Flyest: *As used in the book, to look and feel like the greatest i.e. best dressed, nicest car.*

Fresh or Freshest: *When talking about clothes, or any material tangible item, to have the best of what is available. To look like good or look your best.*

Game Spitter: *Someone who talks from experience about the business they are in and put it in a form of a rap.*

Hold(ing) Something: *To borrow or ask someone for something.*

Hooking Up: *Two people getting together sexually without knowing much about each other.*

Hydro: *A type of marijuana growing process and a certain strain.*

IJS: *I'm Just Saying*

Indo: *A type of marijuana strain.*

Juice: *Having power and/or control in the streets.*

Jump Off: *A sexual relationship with someone you do not take seriously or see a future in.*

Jump-Out Boys: *Police Drug Task Force officers*

Jux: *A criminal act, typically a robbery.*

Lean: *Is a drug concoction made of liquid promethazine and codeine being mixed into a sugary drink.*

Loud: *Very strong marijuana with high levels of THC. Typically, it is called loud because of the strong smell.*

Macking: *A form of pimping where making a profit is not necessarily the end goal. It is more about being able to have plenty of sexual partners without any commitment to any particular one.*

MP3: *A device used to play music.*

Mumble Rap: *Garbled sounding lyrics over slowed down beats*
Off-The-Porch: *Indicates that someone has been living the street life from a very young age.*

OG: *Original Gangster*

Pick Me: *Typically, women who put extras on things so that men can choose them over other women.*

Pimping: *A person, usually a guy, who promotes the selling of women for sex in exchange for protection and mental guidance.*

Potnas: *A play on the word "Partner" used especially by New Orleans natives.*

Pullout Game: *The ability to release from your sexual partner before ejaculation.*

Pussy Popping: *A provocative looking dance done by females that requires them to protrude their derriere in a sexual manner.*

Reggie: *A euphemism for a regular strain of marijuana.*

Reppin: *A slang version of the word representing. It means to represent something you are supporting.*

Riding: *To fully support the ideals and opinions of something or someone.*

Scattered-Sites: *A type of government housing that resembled small housing projects in the ghetto.*

Scoring: *Buying drugs to resale.*

Second Lines: *In New Orleans, a neighborhood parade that is comprised of a small brass band walking and playing music throughout the community. Second line parades are usually associated with celebrating the dead.*

Set-Tripping: *Usually in gang culture when one is thoroughly representing where they are from in another neighborhood. Or, being in another hood that you are not welcomed in.*

Shiny Suit Era: *An era in hip-hop that focused on overly decadent everything: fashion, cars, beat selection, etc.*

Simp: *The opposite of a pimp. Someone who allow women to take advantage of him, disrespect him, and use him for financial gain. Someone always coming to the aid of a woman regardless of her transgressions.*

Skeet: *To ejaculate into a woman without protection. Or simply to ejaculate.*

Sneak Dissing: *Subtle, yet intentional subliminal messages put in a song aimed at a specific person.*

Spittin: *When someone is rhyming or rapping well.*

Stickup Kid: *A person who robs others at gunpoint.*

Streaming: *A new way to listen to music of your favorite artists through an app. Search Streaming Services.*

Street Pharmacist: *A local drug dealer.*

Syrup: *Another name for lean. See lean definition.*

Truck Jewelry: *Large gold jewelry, particular, rope chains worn by rappers in the Foundational and Golden eras.*

Twerk: *A provocative looking dance done by females that requires them to protrude their derriere in a sexual manner.*

Wannabe: *A person pretending to be something they are not.*

Weight: *A lot of drugs for resale.*

Work: *Any type of drugs that can be resold.*

Vinyl LP (12-inch and 7-inch aka 45s): *A thin round vinyl medium that music was recorded to. Also called records.*

Y2k: *The year 2000. Also, an ideal that all computers were going to shut down once the year 2000 rolled in, thus causing the world to end.*

If there are any words, terms, or phrases that the reader is not familiar with; and it is not present in the above glossary, please email author at: info@vlcollinsjr.com if you have any questions. The author will answer you with his meaning and intent of what you are questioning.

BIBLIOGRAPHY

Associated Press. "First Cell phone a true 'brick'." Nbcnews.com, April 11, 2005. http://www.nbcnews.com/id/7432915/ns/technology_and_science-wireless/t/first-cell-phone-true-brick/

Belafonte, Harry, Steven Hager, Andy Davis, Afrika Bambaataa, and Melle Mel. *Beat Street*. VHS. United States: ORION Pictures Corp., 1984.

Bellis, Mary. "Meet the Men Who Created the MP3." ThoughtCo, August 9, 2019. https://www.thoughtco.com/history-of-mp4-1992132.

Bradshaw, Jon. *80 Blocks from Tiffany's. 80 Blocks from Tiffany's*. USA: Above Average Productions Inc., 1979. 80 Blocks.

Braithwaite, Fred. *Wild Style*. VHS. USA: 3DD Entertainment, 1982.

Breakin' - the Street Dance. Film. USA: MGM, 1984.

Breakin' 2 - Electric Boogaloo. Film. USA: MGM, 1984.

Callas, Brad. "The Fifteen Best Hip-Hop Covers of All Time." Medium.com, February 1, 2017. https://medium.com/@bradcallas/the-15-best-hip-hop-album-covers-of-all-time-5b0031b6571d

Charity, Justin, Damien Scott, Rob Kenner, Angel Diaz, Russ Bengtson, C. Vernon Coleman, and Frazier Tharpe. "The Best Rap Song, Every Year Since 1979." Complex. Complex, July 8, 2015. https://www.complex.com/music/best-rap-songs-since-1979/.

Chepkemoi, Joyce. "What Was the Y2K Scare?" WorldAtlas.

WorldAtlas, August 1, 2017. https://www.worldatlas.com/articles/what-was-the-y2k-scare.html.

Gangs of New York. Film. Milano: Twentieth century fox, 2003.

Gershon, Livia. "How Stereotypes of the Irish Evolved From 'Criminals' to Cops." History.com. A&E Television Networks, December 18, 2017. https://www.history.com/news/how-stereotypes-of-the-irish-evolved-from-criminals-to-cops.

Gov, CDC. "Adolescents and Young Adults." Centers for Disease Control and Prevention. Centers for Disease Control and Prevention, December 7, 2017. https://www.cdc.gov/std/life-stages-populations/adolescents-youngadults.htm.

Harris, Mark. "How to Stream Music and Songs to Your Computer or Mobile Device." Lifewire, March 9, 2020. https://www.lifewire.com/what-is-streaming-music-2438445.

Herbert, Tim. "History of the Acadians." Acadian-Cajun.com, January 1, 1997. http://www.acadian-cajun.com/hisacad1.htm

History.com Editors, History.com. "U.S. Immigration Timeline." History.com. A&E Television Networks, December 21, 2018. https://www.history.com/topics/immigration/immigration-united-states-timeline

Hughes, Allen, Allen Hughes, Albert Hughes, Albert Hughes, and Tyger Williams. *Menace II Society*. *Menace II Society*. New Line Cinema, 1993. Menace II Society (1993).

Katz, Nikki. "Black Women are the most Educated Group in the U.S." June 20, 2020. https://www.thoughtco.com/black-women-most-educated-group-us-4048763

Lineberry, Cate. "Tattoos." Smithsonian.com. Smithsonian Institution, January 1, 2007. https://www.smithsonianmag.com/history/tattoos-144038580/.

Orgera, Scott. "How to Hide Your Number with *67." Lifewire.com, March 17, 2020. https://www.lifewire.com/hide-your-number-with-star-67-4154833

NCS. "Who Are the Bloods & Crips: What They Stand For & How They Started: The NCS." National Crime Syndicate. National Crime Syndicate, August 7, 2019. https://www.nationalcrimesyndicate.com/who-are-the-bloods-and-crips/.

Neely, Tim. "The History of Vinyl Records." Our Pastimes, April 12, 2017. https://ourpastimes.com/history-vinyl-records-5373550.html.

Rothman, Wilson. "Beeper Code: The Caveman Days of Text Messaging." Gizmodo.com, December 20, 2009. https://gizmodo.com/beeper-code-the-caveman-days-of-text-messaging-5430493

Rouse, Margaret. "What Is 8-Track Tape? - Definition from WhatIs.com." SearchStorage. TechTarget, September 21, 2005. https://searchstorage.techtarget.com/definition/8-track-tape.

Singleton, John. *Boyz'n the Hood*. *Boyz n the Hood*. Columbia Pictures, 1991. Boyz n the Hood (1991).

Waniata, Ryan. "Remembering the Rise (and Final Fall) of the Late, Great Compact Disc." Digital Trends. Digital Trends, February 9, 2018. https://www.digitaltrends.com/features/the-history-of-the-cds-rise-and-fall/.

ABOUT THE AUTHOR

Acknowledged by his peers as a skillful and creative writer, V.L. Collins Jr. is poised to be the 21st century's most prolific content creator. As Rap, A Juxtaposition of the Eras, is his first published piece of literature, it is his third book that he has written. His second, yet to be titled book, is completed, and will be released next year. The untitled book is written as a narrative that follows the life of a young musician in New Orleans. This book will be the first in a series that will build upon the storyline. V.L. Collins Jr. is also an emcee who is part of a 3-man group made up of him and his two brothers. The group currently performs under the names: Southcidal or the S.O.T.'s (Soldiers Of Truth). He performs under the rap moniker Profhit (PROFessional HIT) and still loves to write rap music for others. Currently, he is writing two screenplays that he is looking to transform into motion picture films.

V.L. Collins Jr. Resources

Web Site

For more information about the work of V. L. Collins Jr., please visit his website at:
www.vlcollinsjr.com

Books by V. L. Collins Jr.

Rap: A Juxtaposition of the Eras

Music featuring the author

Search Southcidal or S.O.T. on all streaming platforms

R.I.P.'S

Yella Boy, Magnolia Slim aka Soulja Slim, Tre-8, Tim Smooth, MC Thick, Pimp Daddy, Kilo G, Magnolia Shorty, G. Slim, Pimp C., Tupac, Prodigy, Biggie Smalls, Big L, Big Pun, Easy E, Nate Dogg, Bushwick Bill, DJ Screw, Guru, Mac Dre, Nipsey Hussle, Sean Price, Pop Smoke, Freaky Tah, Heavy D, Jam Master Jay, Left Eye, Proof, Fat Pat, MCA, DJ Scott La Rock, Mausberg, Mr. Cee, Kadafi, VL Mike, Young Greatness, Huey, XXXTentacion, Bankroll Fresh, 3-2, Bad Azz, Hussein Fatal, 5th Ward Weebie, DJ Black N Mild, Malik B, MC Breed, Fred the Godson, Old Dirty Bastard, Sporty T, VL Mike, Mac Miller, Craig Mack, Juice WRLD, Shawty Lo, Fredo Santana, Camouflage, A$AP Yams, Doe B, The Human Beatbox.

To any deceased person in the hip-hop rap community that I forgot to include, I am truly sorry. I will include you all in the reprinting of this book.

www.ingramcontent.com/pod-product-compliance
Lightning Source LLC
LaVergne TN
LVHW051403080426
835508LV00022B/2949